Contents

My Heart's Home	5
The well-stocked French kitchen	8
Introduction	12
Chapter One	15
Marinated goat's cheese	17
Chicken Provençal	18
Tomates farcies	20
Tian de courgettes & tomates	23
Returning from Ardèche (Diary entry)	24
Salade Lyonnaise	29
Salade Auvergnate	32
The perfect steak	34
The 'Welcome to France' steak-frites	37
Crevettes à l'ail	39
Lentil casserole	41
Chocolate-chunk cookies with rosemary &	43

olive oil

Three recipes to transport you to fields of lavender — 45

Strawberry lavender jam — 46

Quatre-quarts with red berries & lavender — 48

Dainty chocolate & lavender cookies — 50

Chapter 2 — 52

Piperade — 53

Poulet Basquaise — 55

A sumptuous meal in Cahors — 57

First trip to Saint-Émilion — 59

Flan de courgettes & tomates cerises — 61

Tomato festival in Marmande (Diary entry) — 63

Sundays in summer — 65

Simple tomato salad — 68

Summer nectarine & mango jam with rose petals — 69

White chocolate creams with a red berry coulis — 71

Strong stomachs and adventurous tastes (Diary entry) — 73

Côtes de porc à la moutarde — 76

Brochettes de porc — 78

Agen prunes: A taste of the sunshine of Le Sud-Ouest — 79

Autumnal salad with bacon-wrapped Agen prunes	81
Brochettes de magret	83
Glace aux pruneaux & Armagnac	85
Salad with chèvre, apple & walnuts	87
First time in Bourgogne	89
Burgundian guinea fowl	93
Visiting Autun	95
More than Côte-d'Or: Discovering the great wines of Burgundy's Côte Chalonnaise	97
The mysterious lake (Diary entry)	103
Chicken in Banyuls	105
Nose-to-tail	108
Chapter 3	111
Salade d'été	112
Poulet en crapaudine	114
Salted caramel ice cream	116
Asparagus & capers tart	118
Marché Victor Hugo: An epicurean dream	120
Soupe froide de courgettes	124
Roast chicken & chickpea salad	126
Lime panna cotta with roasted apricots	128
Memorable meal in Duras	131

Courgette soup with mascarpone & pesto	134
Tartelettes aux fraises	136
The French apéro	139
Tuna rillettes with ras el hanout	141
Cake salé with baby courgettes, chèvre & green olives	142
Pink garlic from Lautrec	144
Sardines with lemon & piment d'Espelette	147
Tomato tarte tatin	149
Radish greens soup	152
Rhubarb & vanilla cake	154
Bistro at home	156
Hamburgers on brioche with bacon & confit d'oignons	159
Cassolette de la mer	161
Moules marinières	163
Pork loin in lavender & mustard sauce	165
Goat's cheese & onion confit tarts	167
Salad with apple, ham & mustard vinaigrette	169
Tarte flambée	171
Moelleux au chocolat	173
About the Author	175

My Heart's Home

Memories & Recipes of France

Paola Westbeek

> *"I had come to the conclusion that I must really be French, no one had ever informed me of this fact. I loved the people, the food, the lay of the land, the civilized atmosphere, and the generous pace of life."*
> —Julia Child

MY HEART'S HOME: MEMORIES & RECIPES OF FRANCE.

Copyright © 2020, by Paola Westbeek.
All rights reserved.

The well-stocked French kitchen

Besides the common ingredients that are fundamental to every well-stocked kitchen (flour, milk, eggs, butter, olive oil, sugar, etc.), here is a list of items you will always need to have on hand if you want to cook and eat like the French!

Goose fat
Grapeseed oil
Walnut oil
Olive oil
Truffle oil
Coarse sea salt (for boiling potatoes, vegetables, pasta)
Fleur de sel or fine sea salt (for all other uses)
Pepper from a mill (I like to fill my Peugeot with a mix of different peppercorns)

Fresh and dried herbs and spices (grow your own herbs in the garden or even in pots on a sunny windowsill)
Bouquet garni
Dijon mustard
Vinegars (red wine, white wine, apple cider, balsamic)
Good quality stock cubes
Garlic
Onions
Shallots
Lemons
Red, rosé and (sweet) white wine
A bottle of champagne or crémant (always one in the fridge, for special occasions and spur-of-the-moment pleasures)
Pastis
Cognac & Armagnac
Crème fraîche
Single cream
Ready-made puff pastry
Vanilla pods and quality vanilla extract
Ground almonds
Olives
Cornichons (great to serve with terrines and charcuterie)
Capers
Tapenade
Canned sardines and mackerel
Dried sausages

Canned rillettes
Different types of fresh charcuterie
Different types of cheeses
Puy lentils and other dried legumes

A few things to keep in mind

- Make sure you read through the recipe a few times before attempting to make it, and remember to set out your ingredients at the beginning. Nothing is worse than realizing you do not have enough of something halfway through the recipe. Do not be afraid of giving a recipe your own interpretation. Creativity and curiosity are key to the pleasures of the table.
- Eggs should be at room temperature. All eggs are medium eggs with an approximate weight of 50-60g.
- A 'knob of butter' is approx. 10g; a 'large knob of butter' is approx. 20g.
- When cooking, use mild olive oil and save the aromatic, extra virgin variety for dressings and as a finishing touch over dishes.
- Use quality sea salt flakes such as fleur de sel or Maldon salt. When adding the salt, grind the flakes finely between your fingers.
- You will notice that ingredients have been listed in metric measurements. I firmly believe that weighing ingredients is the most accurate way to cook and bake and will lead to the best results. All you need is a kitchen scale. I promise, after seeing how it can improve your cooking, you won't want to be without it!

Introduction

When we visit France, we change. I don't think it only has to do with being on vacation. Of course, vacations are all about enjoyment, no matter where the destination. In our case, however, something happens as soon as we load the last piece of luggage into the car's trunk and drive from our house in the Netherlands to our heart's home, France (come summer, more specifically, Duras in Lot-et-Garonne). It feels as though we're driving to a place where life is always good. A place where people slow down and take time to really enjoy the little things. Like a grand crème and a croissant at the local café or a chat with the butcher at the weekly market. People still ask me why we don't choose another place to spend our free time. Why do we always choose France? The answer is quite simple. There is so much of France to see – and we feel at home there. We love France's food and drink culture, and in our hearts, the three of us (four, including our dachshund Charlie, named after Aznavour, of course) feel very French!

There's nothing like floating out of a restaurant after enjoying a three-course lunch with a carafe of local wine. We don't mind getting up early to visit the markets where we buy fresh fruit, good meat, wine straight from the producers and local cheeses. We love lazy drives through the vineyards, both the familiar ones made purely for our own pleasure and the ones made in search of new oenological discoveries. In France, our taste buds awaken. They come to life and shout with excitement!

If you asked me to tell you about some of the most memorable moments we've had in France, I would probably pop open a bottle of wine and ask you to make yourself comfortable. There are so many stories to tell. So many wonderful places, people and experiences that are etched in my memory... and will forever stay in my heart. In the following pages, I would like to give you a peek into our days in France by sharing excerpts from my travel diaries as well as recipes that resulted from those travels. I have included my interpretation of French classics as well as ideas that came to me after a walk through a lavish summer market or a conversation with a local producer.

The memories, stories and recipes of France in the pages ahead are an ode to a country that inspires and amazes me. It is part cookbook and part personal diary of a Francophile. In short, a book meant to transport, delight and entice. I hope my recipes and words about my beloved France will inspire you in many ways.

Chapter One

A Love Story Begins

First Time In Paradise

It was our first vacation in the south of France, and I remember that I had to keep pinching myself. What fascinating beauty and amazing scents! I was convinced we had suddenly taken an unexpected turn and ended up in paradise. Especially on the day we drove from Lamastre in Ardèche to Orange in Vaucluse, taking little breaks along the way to experience new and wonderful things.

We marveled at the rows of fruit and olive trees in Nyons, and I remember stopping by the side of the road to check out a stand selling all kinds of Tanche olive products. There were crates full of cherries for sale, too – dark, plumper than I'd ever seen and with an irresistibly sweet aroma. I purchased a large bag (which the three of us ravenously devoured), a huge bottle of olive oil and a jar of those black, wrinkled, little olives. In Montélimar we treated ourselves to chewy nougat, and in wine towns such as Châteauneuf-du-Pape and Gigondas we bought fabulous, hearty wines.

Hungry, we decided to have dinner in Orange and found the perfect table at restaurant *La Sangria*. A hot, dry wind was blowing through town that afternoon, and if I close my eyes, I can still feel its sensation against my skin – thick and heavy with the faint scent of lavender and thyme. The *plat du jour* was a trio of *légumes farcis* served on a bed of lettuce. A simple and delightful meal full of sunny flavors, deliciously washed down with a glass of light pink rosé. Dessert was a small bowl of silky *fromage blanc* crowned with a tangy *coulis* of red berries.

The food and wine were wonderful, but the best part was the journey that led us to that restaurant: the colors we saw along the way, the things we tasted and the heavenly aromas of a place that would forever stay with me. In my happiest thoughts, I can still escape to that place of unparalleled beauty.

Marinated goat's cheese

In this recipe, soft, creamy goat's cheese is marinated in an aromatic oil flavored with lemon peel, pink peppercorns and fragrant herbs. Both the cheese and the oil are delicious on salads.

Note: Sterilize your jars by boiling them.

Makes: 6 pieces

Ingredients:
125g soft goat's cheese (*chèvre frais*)
4 tbsps chili oil
1 tsp whole, pink peppercorns
2 small dried chilies
Small bunch of thyme
4 pieces of lemon peel (from an unwaxed, organic lemon)
Enough good-quality extra virgin olive oil to fill a jar (approx. 450ml)

Instructions:
Put the cheeses in the jar, add the rest of the ingredients and close tightly. Keep the jar in the fridge for two days before using the cheese and oil.

Chicken Provençal

The French love chicken, In fact, one-quarter of the meat that appears at their table is *poulet*, whether it be roasted for Sunday lunch or cooked into rich stews such as this one. There are many varieties of chicken available in France, from the gourmet *Poulet de Bresse* (you can read about its history in my book *Dishing it Up: The Story behind Twenty Icons of French Food & Drink*) to more affordable birds reared locally and sold by farmers at the market. As with any kind of meat, I advise that you choose quality over quantity and spend your money on a beautiful organic chicken that was raised slowly and with respect. Who wants meat pumped full of water, growth hormones and antibiotics, anyway? Serve this fragrant chicken dish with fluffy white rice and a glass of rosé.

Ingredients:
2 tbsps olive oil
Salt (preferably *fleur de sel*) and fresh pepper
2 chicken quarters
1 large onion, halved and thinly sliced
100ml rosé wine

300g sweet cherry tomatoes, halved
4 garlic cloves, sliced
Small bunch of thyme
70g green olives

Instructions:

Heat the oil in a shallow, heavy-bottomed casserole, season the chicken with salt and pepper and brown on all sides for approx. 8 minutes. Lower the heat, remove the chicken from the pan, place in a dish and cover with foil. Add the onions to the fat left in the pan and sauté for 3 minutes. Stir in the wine and return the chicken to the pan. Scatter with the tomatoes (place them around the chicken, not on top), garlic and thyme. Reduce the heat to a simmer, place a lid on the pan and cook for 35 minutes. Add the olives and cook uncovered for 15 minutes. Serve with rice.

Tomates farcies

When I first tasted stuffed vegetables in Orange, I found the tomatoes the most delicious. With baking, their already sweet flesh seems to become even more plump and fragrant, forming a delectable contrast with the robust flavors and textures of the filling.

In this recipe, I use a combination of ground pork and beef, but I also suggest you try them with sausages, especially *Saucisse de Toulouse*. In that case, though, I would go easy on the seasoning (especially the salt) since the sausages are already packed with flavor.

Serve these stuffed tomatoes over fluffy, steamed white rice or perhaps with some bread on the side. A fruity Beaujolais or a Provence rosé will pair very well with this dish.

Note: To make sure the tomatoes don't topple over while baking, cut a small sliver off their bottoms.

Serves 4

Ingredients:

8 medium-sized tomatoes
1 tbsp mild olive oil
1 shallot, finely chopped
2 garlic cloves, finely chopped
300-350g ground pork and beef mix
40g fresh breadcrumbs (I make my own from slightly stale bread)
2 tsps *Herbes de Provence*
Small handful flat-leaf parsley, chopped
2 tbsps ketchup
2 tbsps pine nuts
1 egg, lightly whisked
Salt (preferably *fleur de sel*) and fresh pepper

Instructions:

Preheat the oven to 200°C and lightly grease a casserole (large enough to hold the tomatoes snuggly) with a little oil. Cut the tops of the tomatoes and hollow them out. Reserve the tops. Sprinkle the inside of the tomatoes with salt and place them upside down on kitchen paper. Heat the olive oil and gently sauté the shallots and garlic for approx. 3 minutes. Put the ground meat in a large bowl together with the breadcrumbs, *Herbes de Provence*, parsley, ketchup, pine nuts, egg, cooked shallots and garlic, and salt and pepper. Combine everything well. Divide the mixture over the hollowed tomatoes, drizzle the dish with olive oil and pop in the oven for approx. 30 minutes. After this time, put the tomato caps back on, and allow the dish to cook for an additional 20 minutes. Serve the tomatoes over steamed white rice, making sure you drizzle each portion with some of the wonderful pan juices.

Tian de courgettes & tomates

A *tian* is a dish that is popular in sunny Provence. You'll need the best tomatoes and courgettes: seasonal and preferably organic.

Serves 4

Ingredients:
6 ripe tomatoes, thinly sliced
1 large courgette, thinly sliced
Herbes de Provence
Salt (preferably *fleur de sel*) and fresh pepper
Good-quality extra virgin olive oil

Instructions:
Preheat the oven to 180°C and lightly grease a round oven dish with a little olive oil. Layer the tomatoes and courgettes in a wheel pattern, slightly overlapping. Season with the *Herbes de Provence* and salt and pepper. Drizzle generously with olive oil and bake for approx. 40 minutes. Drizzle with a little more oil right before serving. This is a fantastic side dish with fish or chicken.

Returning from Ardèche (Diary entry)

Falling in love with France is easy. I have returned more infatuated with the country than ever after enjoying some of the most impressive landscapes, wonderful food and exquisite wines. There is so much I want to tell you, but where do I start! Should I describe the unforgettable afternoon I spent sampling wines with a charming vigneron at *Tain l'Hermitage*? Should I tell you about the fragrant lavender fields that endlessly stretch into azure skies? Or about all the feasting I crammed into two way too short weeks?

Our destination this year was Ardèche, a department located in the Auvergne-Rhône-Alpes region and home to some of the famous Côtes du Rhône wines. The area is known for its picturesque villages, majestic panoramas, lush vineyards – *and chestnuts*! Breakfast with crackers and *crème de marrons* is my new addiction. Absolutely divine! Not to mention what a fantastic drink *crème de chataigne* and white wine make!

We rented a lovely house at the top of a mountain in a tiny village just outside Labatie d'Andaure. I will never forget our gutsy adventure into the village that first day and how we had to wipe the sweat from our brows while driving up the very tight one-lane road that led to our house. We got somewhat used to it after the second day and didn't even mind that it took us half an hour of holding our breath before we reached Lamastre, the nearest city. We drove there almost every day, either for a pastry before our day trips or for lunch at restaurant *Le Châtaignier*. I always ordered either the *Salade Châtaignier*, made with *jambon cru*, spiced *crème fraîche* and whole chestnuts, or a perfectly grilled *entrecôte*: rare, or as they say in France, *saignant*, and not cooked to resemble the texture of a shoe sole.

After lunch, we sometimes headed for a drink at bar *Le Modern* on the *Quai Farconnet*, a lively street on the banks of the Rhône River in Tournon-sur-Rhône. I remember the beautiful view of the Hermitage vineyards before me as I sat there waltzing my wine, staring into the distance and revelling in the moment.

Wine routes were combined with drives through the Drôme Provençale's *Route de la Lavande*. The huge fields of purple lavender against a backdrop of green mountains reaching into those clear, deep blue skies was like nothing I had ever seen. I would step out of the car, breathe deeply and return convinced that this wasn't France – *this was paradise*!

We strolled through the Roman city of Orange (situated in the Vaucluse) and explored the *Theater Antique d'Orange* – one of the three best preserved Roman theaters in the world. Gastronomic day trips included cities such as Le Puy-en-Velay and Lyon.

The trip to the sacred city of Le Puy-en-Velay turned out to be quite exciting. Driving into the city, we noticed the huge statue of Notre-Dame at the top of *Rocher Corneille*. I pointed it out to Hans, and when he suggested we climb to the top, I let out a gasp. Sure enough, the temptation was too big, and once we got there, we bravely made the climb to the summit of the rock which rises 757 meters above sea level. The first stop was the Romanesque cathedral of Notre-Dame – a famous pilgrimage site with architecture dating back from the 5th to the 15th century and the main construction dating to the first half of the 12th century. Next, was the climb up to the actual statue of Notre-Dame: built in 1860 out of 110 tons of bronze that came from 213 melted cannons captured at Sebastopol, she towers over the city at 22.7 meters. We all made it up to the foot of the statue (you should have seen the view of the city from up there!) but only Hans was brave enough to actually go into the statue and make it to her arms. He told me that the sound of the howling wind was pretty scary from up there (my dear husband is not one who gets scared easily). And all of this before I even had a chance to buy my favorite lentils! The reason I had wanted to visit Le Puy-en-Velay in the first place!

In Lyon, the third largest city in France after Paris and Marseille, I visited the market on the banks of the river Saône at *Quai St. Antoine*. A feast to behold! Especially the baskets filled with dark red peppers, fat purple aubergines, fresh courgettes crowned with delicate yellow flowers, herbs and seasonal fruit. One stall was selling shiny olives in all shades of green, black and purple.

After the market, we stopped for lunch on *Rue Mercière*, a street known for its exquisite restaurants. At *Maitre Pierre*, I ordered *quenelles de brochet*, a specialty consisting of a delicate mousse of creamed fish, eggs and butter, poached in bouillon and served with a russet cream sauce. I sighed when the first forkful of this silky, airy delicacy crossed my lips. After a warm *tarte tatin* for dessert, we explored the rest of the city before heading to *Les Halles de Lyon, Paul Bocuse*, an indoor market bursting with an incredible culinary bounty.

At the end of our trip, I came home with eight bottles of wine from the vineyards of Hermitage, Châteauneuf-du-Pape and Gigondas; fat vanilla pods; chestnut everything (liqueur, flour, purée, cookies); fine mustards and spices; nougat; chocolate; olive oil; lentils; fancy salts; colorful Provençal tablecloths; kitchenware; *savon de Marseille* and cookbooks from every area we visited!

Salade Lyonnaise

More filling than a simple green salad, French mixed salads (*salades composées*) are topped with meats, fish, cheese, vegetables, nuts, potatoes and other substantial ingredients. Examples include the *Salade Niçoise* with tuna, haricots verts, olives and hard-boiled eggs; the *Salade Périgourdine*, which when done really well, features sautéed potatoes and hearty specialties from the southwest such as thinly sliced duck breast, foie gras and *gésiers* (duck gizzards); or the *Salade Lyonnaise*, from Lyon, as the name suggests, with frisée lettuce, crisp bacon, a mustardy vinaigrette and a poached egg.

With a glass of Merlot, this salad is guaranteed to transport me back to France any time.

Note: Remember to make sure your lettuce is dry. Nothing will ruin a salad like wet leaves.

Serves 4

Ingredients:
1 tbsp red wine vinegar

½ shallot, finely chopped
Salt (preferably *fleur de sel*) and fresh pepper
1 tsp Dijon mustard
2 tbsps sunflower oil
1 tbsp extra virgin olive oil
100g lardons, cut into strips
8 slices of baguette, cut at an angle
4 handfuls frisée lettuce
4 really fresh eggs
2 tbsps white wine vinegar
Salt (preferably *fleur de sel*) & fresh pepper
Chopped chives, to garnish

Instructions:

Start by making the vinaigrette. Pour the red wine vinegar into a large bowl and add the shallot and some salt and pepper. Whisk in the mustard followed by the oils. Once the mixture emulsifies, it is ready. Fry the lardons in an ungreased frying pan until crisp. In the meantime, place the slices of baguette under a hot grill, turning them once so that the other side also browns. Carefully toss the dry frisée through the dressing making sure the leaves are evenly coated. Drain the bacon and toss through the salad. Divide the salad over 4 plates. To poach the eggs, break them into 4 cups. Do not crack the eggs directly into the water. Once the water is simmering (not boiling!), add the vinegar and whisk in a stirring motion to create a sort of whirlpool effect. Gently drop in your eggs and cook them for 2 ½ to 3 ½ minutes, depending on their size. Remove the eggs with a slotted spoon and place them on kitchen paper to drain well. You can trim the whites if necessary. Place the eggs on the salad and season with fine salt and freshly cracked pepper. Garnish with the chives and serve with the grilled baguette slices and a glass of Merlot.

Salade Auvergnate

I had this *salade composée* on a sweltering summer day at a restaurant in Le Puy-en-Velay, all while thinking it would make a perfect autumn lunch.

Serves 4

Ingredients:
250g lardons
½ romaine lettuce, shredded
½ iceberg lettuce, shredded
1 large, red onion, halved and thinly sliced
150g blue cheese (*bleu d'Auvergne*), crumbled
1 large, sweet pear, cored and chopped
80g walnuts, roughly chopped

For the vinaigrette
4 tbsps extra virgin olive oil
1 tbsp apple cider vinegar
1 tsp honey
1 tsp Dijon mustard
Salt (preferably *fleur de sel*) and fresh pepper

Instructions:
Fry the lardons in an ungreased frying pan over

a medium heat until they are browned and crisp. Drain them and set aside. Whisk the ingredients for the dressing in a large bowl. Add the two kinds of lettuce leaves to the bowl and toss so that everything is coated with the dressing. Divide the dressed lettuce among 4 plates. Top with the onions, cheese, pears, lardons and walnuts.

The perfect steak

I guess you could say that I've become, well, yes, *addicted* to steak. Not just any steak though, but a properly cooked steak. One that's so tender it melts in the mouth. I recently had the misfortune of buying a less than perfect steak and believe me, even though the cooking was perfect, nothing could salvage it, or my jaw, which ached after just a few bites. I was the only one to blame. A typical case of a craving when my trusted butcher was closed.

In fact, that's where a good steak begins – from a good source. Find a knowledgeable butcher who sells high-quality, free-range/organic meat and you're off to a very good start. We can basically consult our butcher for anything or ask for any kind of meat, and he'll gladly help us. *Please, please, please* stay away from those plastic-wrapped meats from the supermarket, unless you're prepared to be disappointed, just like I was when I had a craving and my butcher was closed. I'm not saying that all meat from the supermarket is bad. They have a very decent selection of organic meat these days –

it's just that if you want a good steak, you're better off with a butcher.

Before cooking your steak (we happen to love *bavette*), you'll want it to come to room temperature, so take it out of the fridge at least half an hour before cooking. Keep in mind that the steps I am about to describe are essential if you want juicy, tender results. I know there are issues with leaving meat out of the fridge or undercooking it, but I, for one, have eaten my fair share of steaks prepared this way with no ill effects.

You'll want your **steaks** to be nice and dry, so grab some kitchen paper and dry them off on both sides. Next, heat up a large frying pan and add **one tablespoon of mild olive oil** and **a large knob of good butter** (not margarine or butter for frying, just plain, full-fat, good butter). Season the meat on one side with plenty of **fine sea salt (preferably *fleur de sel*)** and **fresh pepper**. Once the fat is sizzling, add your meat and turn down the heat just a little. I like my meat quite rare, so I'll give each side about **2 to 3 minutes**, depending on the thickness.

Try not to touch the meat while it's cooking. The next step is to turn the meat over. Now whatever you do, do not turn your meat over with a fork! You'll risk losing precious juices! Instead, use a pair of tongs. Make sure you season the other side of the meat and give it the same amount of time as the first side.

If you want, at this point your steak is almost ready

to eat. The hardest part is the **3 to 4 minute resting time**. This ensures that the juices spread out nicely inside the meat.

Once the steaks are cooked, you can make a wine gravy directly in the pan. Simply remove the meat from the pan, put it on a plate and cover with aluminum foil. Lower the heat to medium and add in a **knob of butter** and **½ a finely chopped shallot**. Cook for 2 minutes. Add **a small glass of red wine** to the pan and let it bubble for a minute or two. Swirl in a **small knob of butter** and cook for an extra minute. Pour these heavenly pan juices over the meat and serve with a scattering of parsley. This recipe serves two.

The 'Welcome to France' steak-frites

I am not exactly sure when we started the tradition of ordering *steak-frites* as our first meal when we arrive in France, but it has certainly become something we very much look forward to. Especially in the summer, when we take two days to make our thirteen-hour drive to the southwest, stopping for one night at a hotel somewhere near Vierzon or Orléans. From the moment I step in the car in the quietness of the morning, I start longing for that perfectly grilled steak that will officially welcome me into the country. I order it with a side of fries and a bottle of Bordeaux, and I eat it in blissful anticipation, knowing this is only the beginning.

Though *steak-frites* will always taste best in France, making this bistro classic at home is easy.

Serves 4

Ingredients:
800g floury potatoes, such as Maris Piper

Sunflower oil
2 tbsps olive oil
2 knobs of butter
4 rib-eye steaks (approx. 150g each), dried with kitchen paper and at room temperature
Salt (preferably *fleur de sel*) and fresh pepper

Instructions:

Preheat the oven to 90°C. Cut the potatoes lengthwise into slices of approx. 5mm and then again lengthwise into fries. Rinse with cold water and dry thoroughly with a clean tea towel. Heat the sunflower oil to 140°C and fry the potatoes in two batches for approx. 6-8 minutes per batch, depending on the thickness of the potatoes. Remove from the oil and allow to drain and cool on kitchen paper. Heat 1 tbsp of the oil and 1 knob of butter in a large frying pan. Season one side of the steaks with salt and pepper. Fry the meat for 2-3 minutes on the seasoned side. Season the other side, flip over and cook for another 2-3 minutes. Place the steaks on a tray and keep them warm in the oven while you cook the other two the same way. You can also cook the steaks at the same time if you have two large frying pans. Once done, place in the oven next to the two other steaks. Heat the sunflower oil again to 190°C and fry the potatoes in two batches for approx. 2-3 minutes. Drain thoroughly on kitchen paper and season with plenty of sea salt. Serve with the fries and a salad.

Crevettes à l'ail

One of the nicest ways to cook large, black tiger prawns is with plenty of garlic, chili, a squeeze of lemon and a scattering of freshly chopped parsley. I like to cook and serve them in a fish pan, gloriously bringing it to the table with the sizzling sounds and heavenly aromas. All this meal requires is garlic mayonnaise (one can never have too much garlic), perhaps some baked tomatoes, bread and a bottle of chilled white wine.

Note: Serve with a bowl for the shells, small bowls of lemon water to clean the fingers and plenty of kitchen paper.

Serves 2-3

Ingredients:
4 tbsps olive oil
500g large, fresh, tiger prawns, with shells and tails, but no heads
1 small red chili, chopped
3 garlic cloves, finely sliced
Juice of ½ lemon

Fresh chopped flat-leaf parsley

Instructions:

Heat 3 tbsps of the oil in a large non-stick fish pan or skillet and add the prawns and chili. Cook for 2 minutes, turn the prawns over, then sprinkle with the garlic and cook for an additional minute. Drizzle with the remaining tbsp of olive oil and squeeze in the lemon. Finish with a scattering of parsley and serve immediately.

Lentil casserole

Lentilles vertes du Puy are small, dark green lentils with a slightly nutty flavor. They received the A.O.C. (*Appellation d'Origine Contrôlée*) certification in 1996. Use them in all kinds of salads (they keep their shape after cooking) or try them in this warming casserole.

Serves 4

Ingredients:
1 shallot
2 garlic cloves
1 carrot
1 celery stalk
2 tbsps olive oil
325g Puy lentils, rinsed and checked for stones
400ml water
350ml red wine
1 tsp *Herbes de Provence*
2 bay leaves, dried
Salt (preferably *fleur de sel*) and fresh pepper
8 Merguez sausages
Chopped flat-leaf parsley

For the vinaigrette:
3 tbsps extra virgin olive oil
1 tbsp red wine vinegar
1 tsp Dijon mustard

Instructions:

Mince the shallots, garlic, carrot and celery finely in a food processor. Heat the oil in a heavy-bottomed casserole and add the vegetables. Gently cook for approx. 5 minutes. Stir in the lentils, add the water, wine and seasonings, but not the salt and pepper. Allow this to come to the boil, turn down the heat immediately, cover and allow to gently cook for 30 minutes. Take the lid off the pan, season with salt and pepper, and turn the heat up a little higher. Continue to cook (without the lid this time) while you get on with grilling the sausages. Whisk all the ingredients for the dressing, pour this over the warm lentils and top with the grilled sausages. Sprinkle with the chopped parsley and serve with bread and a salad.

Chocolate-chunk cookies with rosemary & olive oil

On a road trip through the Provence, we decided to stop at a bakery somewhere between Orange and Avignon. I entered the bakery with Kirstie (who's always in for a treat), and she immediately spotted a thick, pale cookie studded with nuggets of chocolate. She had to try them, and of course, so did I.
I ordered six and we shared them as a special treat during the rest of our trip. Little did I know how magical that treat would prove to be because these cookies weren't just any ordinary chocolate chip cookies, but a decidedly Provençal variation with rosemary and peppery olive oil!
From that very first bite, I knew this was a recipe I had to recreate.
Do not even think of serving these cookies with milk! They go best with a glass of Banyuls. Armagnac or a strong, dark espresso.

Makes approx. 20 cookies

Ingredients:

250g all-purpose flour
½ tsp baking powder
Pinch of salt (preferably *fleur de sel*)
1 ½ tsp dried rosemary
120g good-quality, dark chocolate, chopped
2 eggs
65 ml olive oil
1 tsp vanilla extract
200g sugar

Instructions:

Sift the flour and baking powder in a large bowl. Add the salt, making sure to grind it finely between your fingers. Add the rosemary and chopped chocolate and stir well. Whisk the eggs with the olive oil, vanilla extract and sugar. Add the wet ingredients to the dry and stir well with a wooden spoon. Knead the dough a bit with your hands while it's still in the bowl and then shape it into a ball. Divide the dough in half and form a thick disk from each piece. Wrap each piece in cling film and allow the dough to rest in the fridge for at least 1 hour. Overnight is also fine. Make sure to take the dough out of the fridge 10 minutes before rolling it out. Preheat the oven to 180°C and line a baking sheet with baking paper. Roll out the dough on a floured surface and cut out cookies of about 1cm thick and 5cm in diameter. Place them on the baking sheet with a little space between each cookie. Bake the cookies for 20 minutes and allow to cool.

Three recipes to transport you to fields of lavender

Visiting France always fills me with culinary inspiration. I came up with the following lavender recipes after returning from my travels through the Drôme Provençale.

Note: The key to cooking with dried flowers is to use them sparingly. That way the flowers enhance the flavor of food instead of masking it with their intense aromas.

Strawberry lavender jam

My favorite strawberry jam recipe reminds me of France and is my own little tribute to the summer. A friend once said that it "tasted like Provence." What a delightful compliment! You'll love the jam on summer mornings, on a lightly buttered piece of toasted baguette and washed down with a nice bowl of French-pressed coffee.

Note: Make sure to use lavender that is safe for consumption!
Sterilize your jars by boiling them.

Makes approx. 500ml

Ingredients:
600g strawberries, washed and hulled
250g gelling sugar
1 ½ tbsp dried lavender (suitable for cooking)
Juice of ½ a small lemon

Instructions:
Cut the strawberries in half and place them together with the sugar and the lavender in a stainless steel pan. Mash them a little with a potato

masher, but make sure you leave some nice chunks. Add the lemon juice, stir and quickly bring everything to the boil. Lower the heat and allow the jam to cook for approx. 30 minutes, stirring frequently. You'll want the jam to bubble away nicely, but make sure that the heat isn't too high. To check if the jam is ready, drop a teaspoonful onto a cold saucer. The jam should be thick and immediately start to set. Transfer the jam to your sterilized jar and allow to cool before refrigerating.

Quatre-quarts with red berries & lavender

My version of this classic French cake is made with a good handful of dried red berries (cranberries, cherries or strawberries) and a touch of lavender. A beautifully scented, red-speckled, buttery loaf perfect for teatime, *or any time*!

Serves 8

Ingredients:
250g all-purpose flour
Pinch of salt (preferably *fleur de sel*)
1 ½ tsp baking powder
225g soft butter
225g fine sugar
4 eggs
1 tbsp dried lavender (suitable for cooking)
120g dried red berries

Instructions:
Soak the dried berries in hot water for approx. 15 minutes. Drain thoroughly. Preheat the oven

to 165°C. Line a 28cm rectangular cake pan with baking paper. Sift flour and salt into a bowl. Add the baking powder and the lavender and stir thoroughly. In a separate bowl, whip the butter and the sugar until light and fluffy. Beat the eggs in a small bowl and add them little by little to the butter and sugar mixture. Fold in the dry ingredients and the dried berries in two batches, stirring thoroughly after each addition. Pour the batter into the prepared cake pan and bake for approx. 1 hour and 25 minutes or until a toothpick inserted in the center comes out clean. Allow to cool on a wire rack before serving.

Dainty chocolate & lavender cookies

One tablespoon of dried lavender is all you will need to transform a simple chocolate cookie into something beautiful. I always store these thin, crisp treats in my prettiest jar. But in all honesty, I'm afraid they never stay there long!

Makes approx. 40 cookies

Ingredients:
225g butter, softened
200g fine sugar
1 egg, lightly beaten
220g self-raising flour
2 tbsps good-quality cocoa powder
Pinch of salt (preferably *fleur de sel*)
1 tbsp dried lavender flowers (safe for consumption)

Instructions:
Preheat the oven to 180°C and line a cookie sheet with baking paper. Cream the butter and sugar

with a handheld mixer or standing mixer. Add the egg and continue beating. Beat in the flour, chocolate, salt and lavender, making sure that the lavender is evenly distributed. Take small teaspoonfuls of the dough and form them into fat, little discs of approx. 3 ½cm in diameter. Place on the prepared cookie sheet approx. 5cm apart and bake for 15-18 minutes. Carefully transfer the cookies to a wire rack to cool. The cookies will be soft when they come out of the oven but will crisp while cooling.

Chapter 2

Taste Discoveries

Southwest France

I have a soft spot for Le Sud-Ouest. The authentic bastides, quaint villages, rolling hills of bright yellow sunflowers, and amazing food and wine have made this one of my favorite parts of France. The region is like honey for the soul!

There is an enormous bounty of fruits and vegetables such as Marmande tomatoes, the famous Agen prunes, Quercy melons and Perigord strawberries. Other regional products include Bayonne ham, *piment d'Espelette*, oysters from Arcachon, black truffles and all sorts of duck and goose products. *Did I mention the wines yet?*

Piperade

In Pays Basque, colorful dishes are generously seasoned with *piment d'Espelette*. Come the late summer, bunches of the bright red peppers are hung to dry from the facades of houses in the pretty village of Espelette before being ground into a delicately spicy condiment used in regional classics such as *Poulet Basquaise* and *piperade*. With tomatoes, onions and red and green peppers, these dishes reflect the colors of the Basque flag. The addition of Bayonne ham, a regional speciality, is quite common in both.

Piperade is delicious as a light lunch. Especially if served with a chilled, fruity Pinot Noir.

Serves 3

Ingredients:
2 tbsps olive oil
1 large, sweet onion, halved and thinly sliced
2 garlic cloves, finely chopped
1 green bell pepper, sliced
2 red bell peppers, sliced
5 small tomatoes, deseeded and sliced

1 ½ tsp *piment d'Espelette*
Salt (preferably *fleur de sel*)
3 eggs
Bayonne ham
Bread, to serve

Instructions:

Heat the oil and add the onion and garlic. Sauté gently for approx. 3 mins. Add the peppers and allow to cook gently for approx. 5 minutes. Add the tomatoes and season with the *piment d'Espelette* and salt. Cover and allow to cook for 20 minutes. Make three wells in the stewed vegetables and break in the eggs. Cover and cook for approx. 5 minutes. Serve with the Bayonne ham and bread.

Poulet Basquaise

Poulet Basquaise is excellent comfort food on those gloomy end-of-summer days when rain and an ever so slight chill in the air start to slowly start to notice the changing of the seasons.

Serves 4

Ingredients:
4 tbsp olive oil
2 onions, finely chopped
2 garlic cloves, finely chopped
100g Bayonne ham, chopped
2 red bell peppers, sliced
1 green bell pepper, sliced
4 ripe tomatoes, chopped
1 ½ tsp ground *piment d'Espelette* (or to taste)
Pinch of sugar
100ml dry white wine
Salt (preferably *fleur de sel*) and fresh pepper
4 chicken quarters, or 8 drumsticks
Chopped flat-leaf parsley

Instructions:

Heat the olive oil in a large casserole. Add the onions and garlic and gently sauté for approx. 3 minutes. Add the ham and continue to cook for a few more minutes. Add the rest of the ingredients (except the chicken). Bring to the boil, reduce the heat, cover and allow to cook for 40 minutes. Brown the chicken pieces 10 minutes before the end of the sauce's cooking time. Add the chicken to the sauce and allow to cook for an additional 35-40 minutes. Taste and adjust the seasoning if necessary. Serve with potatoes or rice and a scattering of chopped parsley.

A sumptuous meal in Cahors

With imposing architectural masterpieces such as the iconic 14th-century Pont de Valentré bridge (according to legend, the central tower is inhabited by the devil!) or the ancient Cathedral of Saint-Étienne (which dates back to the 12th century and rises over the older part of town), Cahors is a Medieval city full of history and French charm. It is the capital of Quercy, a region in southwest France known for hearty cuisine and dark, masculine wines.

Neither the food nor wines of the area are meant for dieters. I have fond memories of a sumptuous meal at restaurant *Le Palais*, situated smack in the middle of one of the busiest streets, *Boulevard Léon Gambetta*. The *Menu Découverte* started with twelve plump escargots sizzling in little pools of melted garlic butter. My main was a tender *magret de canard*, thinly sliced and topped with a thick, chestnut-colored pepper sauce. It was so large that it could have easily served two, yet in my greediness, I managed to finish it all and even soaked up the last bits of sauce with pieces of bread. Of course,

I wouldn't have managed such a feat if it wasn't for the fact that we had the whole afternoon to linger over that leisurely lunch. Plus, a carafe of inky, broad-chested Cahors wine to wash it down with. Fortunately, dessert was light and refreshing: grilled pineapple and raspberry sorbet with a luscious swirl of *crème anglaise*.

After the meal, we left Cahors happy, with stomachs that were a little too full, and a box of wine that would remind us of that lavish feast.

Note: The cuisine of southwest France is centered around bold, hearty flavors that reflect its peasant traditions. Duck is an emblematic specialty and enjoyed in myriad ways: buttery foie gras is slathered on toasted brioche and seasoned with flakes of *fleur de sel*; thick, juicy *magrets* are beautifully grilled over prunings from the *vigne*; and robust legs are preserved in globs of their own fat, which is then used to fry crisp, garlicky potatoes. *Gésiers* (gizzards) are added to rustic salads along with pretty much all the aforementioned preparations of duck, and pizzas are even topped with thin slices of *magret fumé*.

First trip to Saint-Émilion

When we first planned a trip to Saint-Émilion, I was so excited that I prepared myself for a few tears of happiness upon seeing the village's name on the street signs. Saint-Émilion is one of the oldest wine areas in the Bordeaux region. Its wines, primarily made from Merlot grapes, are incredibly smooth and easy to drink. To me they are the most feminine wines of this region

But there's more than wine to make my heart flutter when it comes to Saint-Émilion. Our very first trip started with a drive through the vineyards. We went from one vineyard to the next, Hans getting out of the car to take pictures and I to allow myself the incredible pleasure of cupping my hands around bunches of juicy grapes. When we arrived at the *centre-ville*, I felt as though I had been transported back to the Middle Ages. The village is intersected by steep, cobblestoned streets lined with all sorts of wine and souvenir shops. It was the height of the summer, and masses of tourists were admiring the impressive ruins, walking around with boxes of wine or seeking refreshment at the many lively terraces.

After a stroll through the village and a few wine purchases complete with tastings and wine chats, we decided to round off the afternoon with lunch at the panoramic terrace of *Bistrot Le Clocher*, a restaurant situated at the foot of the largest monolithic church in France. We opted for the *trio de cote d'agneau* served with a mini-flan of minced vegetables and a glass of their best *Grand Cru*. It was a light yet satisfying lunch.

Before heading back to the car, we popped into the famous Ferlion Macarons Blanchez bakery where we purchased Saint-Émilion's gastronomic specialty – macarons! Not the colorful ones with the creamy/jammy fillings, but the flatter, paler ones baked directly onto a piece of parchment paper. These chewy, almondy treats were the sweet ending to one of our most anticipated wine trips.

Flan de courgettes & tomates cerises

These individual flans are great as a side dish to meat or fish, but you can also double the amount of cheese and serve them with a salad as a light vegetarian lunch.

Serves 4

Ingredients:
Knob of butter and a little olive oil
1 medium sweet onion, finely chopped
1 medium courgette, halved and sliced
2 eggs
200ml *crème fraîche*
50ml milk
1 tsp dried basil
20g freshly grated Parmesan
Salt (preferably *fleur de sel*) and fresh pepper
8 cherry tomatoes

Instructions:
Preheat the oven to 180°C and oil your molds.

I used shallow molds for *crème catalane*. Heat the olive oil and butter and gently cook the onion for approx. 5 minutes. Add the courgettes and cook for an additional 3 minutes. In a large bowl, whisk the eggs, *crème fraîche*, milk, basil, Parmesan, salt and pepper. Divide the cooked vegetables over the molds and top with the batter. Finish with the sliced cherry tomatoes and bake for approx. 30-35 minutes.

Tomato festival in Marmande (Diary entry)

After a croissant and a lazy *grand crème*, we decided to leave for Marmande to check out the market and buy some of those gorgeous Marmande tomatoes. They're my favorite. More sweet than tart, plump and full of sunshine.

Unfortunately, when we arrived in the *centre-ville*, we were quite disappointed. No market. Instead of leaving, though, we walked through the city and enjoyed the weather.

Well, it turned out to be our lucky day...

As we approached *Place Clemenceau*, it became evident that something exciting was happening. In the distance, I could spot a few market stalls and lots of people. What were they selling? What was the occasion?

I turned the corner and saw the largest tomato tart ever! It was glistening with ruby-red tomato slices and dotted with black and green olives. It looked so good! The other stands were offering all kinds of products – from preserves to fresh Marmande to-

matoes to regional wine. I was overjoyed!
We had ended up at the annual Marmande Tomato Fiesta!
We purchased three pieces of that irresistible tart, grabbed a table at brasserie *Les Neuf Fontaines*, ordered large glasses of the local white wine and had the most delicious lunch ever – right there, under the glow of the warm French sunshine.

Sundays in summer

The village of Issigeac in Dordogne has narrow streets, authentically preserved architecture and houses with pretty shutters in dusty shades of yellow, cream, gray and brown. When you wander through its streets, you feel as though you're back in the Middle Ages.

Although very busy, especially during the summer, Issigeac's Sunday market is really something that should not be missed. It is definitely one of the most colorful and folkloric in the region, but you do need to be very patient though, as the masses of people will literally force you to walk at the most leisurely of paces. In other words, this market isn't really something you'll want to (or are able to) rush through. And if you have a small dog, like we do, it might be smart to pick it up and carry it safely away from all those scary feet!

Sometimes, when we are lucky enough to find a free table, we stop for a drink and a bit of people-watching at La P'tite Treille, an idyllic little restaurant with its terrace situated under a roof of grapevines. Sitting here sipping something wonderful is absorbing the essence of France in every fiber of your being.

I usually keep my purchases to a minimum at the market. Mainly because we always drive to Soumensac (an even smaller village about half an hour to the west) for lunch afterward, and it isn't a smart idea to leave food in the car when the temperatures outside are above 30°C. I do like to take home some nice Marmande tomatoes, a few boxes of fragrant strawberries and a sweet Quercy melon or two.

The Issigeac market is a great place to start the Sunday, while Soumensac's *Marchés des Producteurs* is the only way to roll into an unforgettable afternoon. On a beautiful hilltop, vendors sell and prepare regional specialties. You'll find just about every kind of duck product (from skewers with duck breasts to terrines of foie gras), all kinds of barbecued meats, some of the fattest escargots, fresh salads made with seasonal vegetables, refreshing fruit desserts, *crêpes*, fresh bread and of course, plenty of wine.

Long tables are set out under the tall trees, and if you want, you can even set your table with your own pretty tablecloth and tableware. The soft, dappled light, the colorful scenery, the foliage of the trees and the beautiful hats worn by most of the people sometimes make me feel as though I'm inside a Renoir painting, especially after my husband took a picture there one summer which will always remind me of one of my favorite masterpieces, Renoir's *Le déjeuner des canotiers*.

Simple tomato salad

This isn't really a recipe. Consider it advice on how to make a fine salad with just a few ingredients. You will need the best summer tomatoes (preferably Marmande), shallots, zingy extra virgin olive oil, a dash of fresh pepper and a sprinkle of *fleur de sel*. I ate this salad for the first time at the Sunday market in Soumensac. There is a salad stand that works magic with perfect seasonal vegetables.

Simply slice your tomatoes very thinly and arrange them on a big plate. Top with paper-thin slices of shallots, a generous drizzle of olive oil, *fleur de sel* and a little pepper. That's all there is to it! One thing to keep in mind, though: never, *ever* try this when tomatoes are not in season and never, *ever* store your tomatoes in the fridge!

Summer nectarine & mango jam with rose petals

This is a recipe guaranteed to make every day feel like a summer Sunday in France.

Makes 1 liter

Ingredients:
1 ripe mango, peeled and chopped
6 ripe nectarines, peeled and chopped
500g gelling sugar
2 tbsps rosewater
1 tbsp dried rose petals (it is essential that you get petals suitable for consumption and NOT sprayed with chemicals)

Note: Sterilize your jars by boiling them.
To peel the nectarines, make an X with a sharp knife on the underside of the fruit before immersing them in boiling water for 2-3 minutes. Rinse under cold water. The skins should peel off easily.

Instructions:
Put all the ingredients in a heavy-bottomed pan,

stir well and allow to cook on medium heat for approx. 45 minutes, stirring occasionally. Let stand for 10 minutes before ladling into jars.

White chocolate creams with a red berry coulis

This creamy, white chocolate dessert is the perfect way to end a Sunday lunch. The red berry *coulis* tastes like sunshine!

Serves 4

Ingredients:
100g white chocolate
300g Greek yogurt
250g strawberries, hulled and chopped
100g red currants
2 tbsps sugar
½ tbsp Kirsch
Mint leaves and fresh fruit, to serve

Instructions:
Gently melt the chocolate au bain-marie. Allow it to cool for a minute and stir in the yogurt until you have a smooth consistency. Divide the cream over four glasses and allow to set in the fridge for a few hours. To make the *coulis*: Put the strawberries,

currants, sugar and Kirsch in a pan. Allow this to come to the boil and immediately reduce the heat. Cook for 10-15 minutes making sure you mash all the fruit as it cooks. The sauce should be thin and not have the consistency of jam. Leave to cool before refrigerating. To serve, pour the *coulis* over each cream and decorate with the mint and fresh fruit.

Strong stomachs and adventurous tastes (Diary entry)

We decided to trust the advice written in the little guest book we found in the house we had rented that summer and headed to a restaurant serving a three-course lunch (complete with a bottle of wine!) for only twelve euros. A bargain! What kind of meal that would be, was anyone's guess, but for that price, I definitely wasn't expecting too much. I was, however, extremely curious.

From the outside, the place looked deserted. The weather was beautiful, yet not a single table at the terrace was occupied. An obvious sign of trouble, I thought. But we were brave, and agreeing to give the place a chance, took a seat at one of the empty tables.

After ten minutes of waiting, I decided to send Hans inside to see if they were serving lunch. They were, but they were not about to serve us outside, considering the heat. We were escorted to the back of the restaurant by a gal with a raspy voice, red lipstick (on the teeth more than on the lips) and dishevelled hair. I braced myself as I followed her, passing the bar full of sweaty men sitting in a cloud of cigarette smoke. The wine was already waiting at the table, open and in a bottle without a label. The only thing I knew was that it was red.

We sat down, poured ourselves a glass and contemplated what was happening around us. There was an older couple to our right. They were finishing some sort of salad, slurping their water (the wine was untouched) and not really saying much to each other. The tables in front of us, on the other hand, were occupied by chatty groups of men (slightly better looking than the ones at the bar), greedily carving into their meat with their own Opinel knives. It was fun to sit there and try to figure out what they were talking about. And hey, the wine wasn't even that bad!

I noticed the large French windows shaded by thin curtains yellowed by cigarette smoke. There were other waitresses walking around, and the peculiar atmosphere combined with their nonchalance suddenly made me feel unusually at home. And the more wine I drank, the stronger that feeling became.

Half a bottle later, the messy-haired waitress came back to announce that the *plat du jour* was *côtes de porc à la moutarde* and informed us that unfortunately, the starter was finished. It was a bit of a disappointment, but at that point I was just happy there was actually going to be any eating.

By the time the garlic-smothered chops arrived, the wine was almost finished. Happily we tucked in, not minding at all that for the rest of the day, our breath would keep us from saying a single word to anyone (except each other).

Halfway through the meal, I remember looking at Hans and asking him what he thought about the meat. He didn't say much and instead poured me the last bit of wine, which came with a complimentary dead fly. That didn't seem to bother me, though. *Seriously, has anyone ever died from an innocent little fly? And doesn't wine prevent gastric upset anyway?*

When we left the restaurant, it was a little after two in the afternoon. I really can't remember much about the rest of the day except that my head was spinning and that every pore in my body was wreaking of garlic. Only later did Hans and I confess to each other that we were glad we were spared a serious bout of food poisoning.

Côtes de porc à la moutarde

Those garlicky pork chops sure caused an impression on us! This version doesn't have half as much garlic, but if you're brave (and have nowhere to go for a few days), go ahead and double the quantities.

Serves 3

Ingredients:
2 tbsps mild olive oil
2 small onions, finely chopped
2 fat garlic cloves, finely sliced
3 pork chops
1 generous glass of dry white wine
250g chestnut mushrooms, sliced
125ml single cream
2 tsps grainy mustard
2 tsps dried tarragon
Salt (preferably *fleur de sel*) and fresh pepper

Instructions:
Heat 1 tbsp of the oil in a frying pan and sauté the onions and garlic for 2-3 minutes. Set aside. Add the other tbsp of oil to the pan, season the chops

with salt and pepper and fry them for approx. 3 minutes on each side. Add the wine, scrape any brown bits, add the onions and garlic and lower the heat. Place a lid on the pan and cook the chops for 15 minutes. Add the mushrooms, cream, mustard and tarragon. Make sure the mustard is fully mixed with the cream. Allow the dish to cook for an additional 5 minutes. Taste, correct the seasoning and serve.

Brochettes de porc

These tasty skewers are perfect for the barbecue or grill. You'll want to marinate the meat well in advance. Go ahead and use your fingers to rub the marinade into the meat.

Serves 3-5

Ingredients:
550g pork shoulder, cubed
1 tbsp dried oregano
1 tsp whole pink peppercorns
Juice of ½ a lemon
1 ½ tbsp chili oil
Salt (preferably *fleur de sel*)

Instructions:
Put all the ingredients in a bowl. Rub the marinade into the meat using your hands. Allow to marinate for 3-5 hours or overnight. Thread the meat through the skewers and grill for approx. 15-20 minutes. Serve with slices of lemon.

Agen prunes: A taste of the sunshine of Le Sud-Ouest

Sweet, glossy and bursting with flavor, Agen prunes have been part of southwest France's gastronomic history since the 12th century. During that time, crusaders returned from Syria with Damson plum trees which the Benedictine monks of Clairac, not far from Agen, crossed with their own, local plum variety. The result was a new kind of plum which they called the *Ente* plum. Since then, the plum has been used to produce the famous *pruneaux d'Agen*, named after the city from which the prunes were shipped all over Europe. Today, more than half of the production of the fruit is still taking place in the Lot-et-Garonne.

The dark plums are harvested between mid-August and mid-September. By that time, they are so ripe and sun-drenched that the trees either naturally drop the fruit or need nothing more than a gentle shake to let them fall into the harvesting nets. After careful sorting, the best fruits are dried and preserved for year-round use.

Agen prunes are not only delicious, but they are also extremely healthy and versatile. Full of fiber, iron and antioxidants, they can be eaten as a nutritious snack or incorporated into a wide variety of recipes. Try them in your oatmeal or cereals, in hearty cold-weather stews and in desserts. The following recipes are an ideal way to enjoy these delicious sweet treats.

Autumnal salad with bacon-wrapped Agen prunes

Serve this autumnal salad as a light lunch or adjust the quantities and offer it as a starter to a main course of duck or chicken.

Serves 4

Ingredients:
For the dressing:
1 tbsp balsamic vinegar
3 ½ tbsps grapeseed oil
½ tsp grainy mustard
1 tsp honey
Salt (preferably *fleur de sel*) and fresh pepper

For the salad:
80g whole almonds
10 slices of bacon, halved
20 *pruneaux d'Agen*
12 slices of French bread
90g soft, fresh goat's cheese, such as Chavroux
200g mixed salad leaves

12 slices of thin, dry-cured ham

Instructions:

Preheat the oven to 220°C and line a baking tray with baking paper. Roast the almonds in an ungreased frying pan, chop them up roughly and set aside. Wrap half a slice of bacon around each prune, secure with a toothpick and place on the baking tray. Pop in the oven for 10-12 minutes, turning the prunes halfway through the cooking time. Remove from the tray and spread out the oils released by the bacon over the tray. Spread the goat's cheese over the bread and place on the tray with the bacony oils. Return to the oven for an additional 4-6 minutes. Keep an eye on the bread and make sure it doesn't burn. In a large bowl, whisk all the ingredients for the dressing. Add in the mixed salad leaves and toss to coat. Divide the salad among 4 plates. Top each plate with the almonds, the ham and the cheese toasts. Place the bacon-wrapped prunes around the sides of the salad and serve immediately. I like this salad accompanied by a smooth, fruity Merlot.

Brochettes de magret

These hearty *brochettes de magret* combine three of the ingredients that southwest France is known for: duck, *pruneaux d'Agen* and Armagnac. They are incredibly easy to make and are perfect for a quick, filling lunch. Cook the skewers over a hot grill or on the barbecue, taking care to turn them frequently so that the sugars in the fruit don't burn. A green salad and perhaps some good bread is all you'll need to serve alongside. Of course, wine is essential. Choose a full-bodied Madiran or a Pomerol.

Makes 4-6 *brochettes*, depending on the size of your skewers

Ingredients:
18 *pruneaux d'Agen*
2 tbsps Armagnac
1 large orange, sliced and cut into small triangles
2 sprigs of rosemary
1 tsp salt (preferably *fleur de sel*)
2 tsps pink peppercorns
2 duck breasts of about 200-250g each, cut into large cubes

Instructions:

Soak the prunes in the Armagnac for at least 30 minutes. Finely chop the rosemary, pink peppercorns and salt. You want to end up with a fine spice rub. Divide the rub in two equal amounts. Sprinkle half of the rub over the pieces of duck. Thread on skewers starting with an orange section, then a piece of duck and then a prune. Finish off with an orange section. Before grilling the *brochettes*, squeeze a little orange juice over them and sprinkle with the rest of the rub. Grill to your liking, taking care to turn the brochettes frequently.

Glace aux pruneaux & Armagnac

Forget the usual rum-raisin variety, the flavor of this Armagnac-infused ice cream is definitely more elegant. Served with an espresso, it makes the perfect ending to your meal. Or serve a single *boule* over a warm *moelleux au chocolat* for a taste of southwest France!

Makes approx. 1 liter

Ingredients:
15 *Pruneaux d'Agen*, chopped
105ml Armagnac
800ml cream
1 vanilla pod, split in half and seeds scraped out
4 egg yolks
170g fine sugar

Instructions:
Soak the chopped prunes in 75ml of Armagnac overnight. The following day, gently cook the prunes and the rest of the Armagnac (in a covered saucepan) for approx. 3 minutes. Allow to cool. Place the cream, vanilla seeds and vanilla pod in

a large saucepan. Heat gently for 3 minutes taking care not to boil the cream. Remove from the heat, remove the vanilla pod and set aside. Beat the egg yolks and the sugar until pale and creamy. Add a little of the egg mixture to the cream and whisk well. Pour the rest of the eggs into the saucepan with the cream, start whisking immediately and return to the heat. Cook over a very low heat, whisking constantly. Once the mixture is thickened (10-15 minutes) remove from the heat, stir in prunes and Armagnac and pour into a bowl set over iced water. Allow to cool and refrigerate overnight. Churn (in batches if necessary) in an ice cream machine.

Salad with chèvre, apple & walnuts

This salad is delicious as a light lunch or starter. The warm, creamy goat's cheese pairs wonderfully with the crisp, juicy slices of apple. Serve the salad with a refreshing Sancerre.

Serves 2

Ingredients:
For the dressing:
1 tbsps Dijon mustard
3 tbsps sunflower oil
1 tbsp red wine vinegar
2 tsps honey
Salt (preferably *fleur de sel*) and fresh pepper

For the salad:
a handful of roughly chopped walnuts
30g lardons
10 mini-*tomme de chèvres*
A few handfuls of mixed salad leaves
1 crisp apple, cored and sliced

Instructions:
Whisk all the ingredients for the dressing in a large bowl. Roast the walnuts in an ungreased frying pan and set aside. Fry the lardons without adding any oil or fat. Drain in a colander lined with strong kitchen paper. Put the cheeses on a baking tray lined with baking paper and grill them under a hot grill for approx. 3-5 minutes. Toss the salad leaves in the bowl with the dressing and then divide them between the plates. Dress each plate with the roasted walnuts, the sliced apple, the lardons and the warm cheeses. Serve immediately.

First time in Bourgogne

It was in the heart of France, Bourgogne, that I developed a true appreciation for wine. One afternoon, while touring through the region's *Route des Grands Crus*, we decided to stop at a little wine shop in Nuits-Saint-Georges, one of the many prestigious wine towns along the famous sixty-kilometer route. Before entering the shop, I had no idea what *terroir* meant and cared little about pairing wine with food. I was a wine novice who only sipped white wine occasionally, and if it was sweet, all the better. Little did I know how much one delectably memorable wine tasting experience would change my life.

I sampled a range of wines, and with each one, I was given a thorough explanation about its origins, vintage and the best foods to pair it with. A whole new world opened up to me from that moment on. At restaurants, I began to ask for wines that complemented my food, and when we traveled through France, no vineyard or wine village was safe from my oenological hunger. I had to get out of the car to dig my hands into the soil, touch the grapes and feel the essence of wine with my fingertips.

Wine wasn't the only thing that caused an impression on me during that trip. The weather was glorious and the landscape lush and green. We stayed at a charming holiday home in the *Parc Naturel Régional du Morvan*, a quiet and peaceful nature reserve dating to 1970 and home not only to farmlands, lakes, woodlands and hills, but also to more than one hundred towns and villages spread out through the departments of Yonne, Nièvre, Saône-et-Loire and Côte-d'Or. The house was small but comfortable, and our daughter Kirstie, who was about five, had a room full of toys, swings overlooking the hills, and even a horse and a pony to pet right from her bedroom window every morning.

We spent many afternoons exploring cities and villages, and stopping along the way to visit churches and museums or to have a drink at a pretty terrace. In Beaune we visited *L'Hôtel-Dieu*, a former hospital for the poor that was built by Nicolas Rolin (chancellor to the Duke of Burgundy, Philippe le Bon) in 1433. At the time, Beaune had greatly suffered from war and famine, and Rolin ensured patients received only the best care. *L'Hôtel-Dieu*, which became a prominent statement of wealth and grandeur, has a splendid courtyard with roofs covered in glazed multicolored tiles arranged in extraordinary geometric patterns. For me, the main attraction was *The Last Judgement Polyptych* by Rogier van der Weyden (1446-1452), one of the most respected artists of the 15th century. This exceptional masterpiece is housed in a dark, cool room which somehow makes its bright colors all the more impressive. It was one of the most captivating paintings I had ever seen, and I found it nearly impossible to turn my back and walk away from it. When we planned the trip to Bourgogne, one of the things I looked forward to most, however, was the food. I could not wait to sink my teeth into a Charolais beef steak, try the famous *boeuf bourguignon* or devour a dish of garlicky snails. I enjoyed wonderful cheeses such as the orange-crusted Époisses bathed in Marc de Bourgogne, and every morning started with fresh bread and pastries from the *boulangerie*. On Wednesdays, we shopped at the weekly market in Autun, an attractive city with Gallo-Roman origins. Landmarks that attest to this are the Roman Amphitheatre (built by Emperor Augustus and known to have been the largest in the Roman world) and the two ancient gateways, the *Porte d'Arroux* and the *Porte St-André*, dating back to the 1st and 4th century respectively. At the market, held around the *mairie*, I would fill my basket with bags of ripe nectarines, apricots, grapes, *tomates coeur de boeuf*, fresh spices, hearty slices of *jambon persillé* (parsleyed ham in aspic, a regional specialty) and honey made by the local bees in the Morvan. And because there was a wonderful brasserie, *Le Commerce*, right across from the market, we would have lunch with the locals before return-

ing to the house for an utterly delightful siesta.
The food, landscapes, wines and people – in the years that followed, that first trip to Bourgogne would lure me to the region time and time again.

Burgundian guinea fowl

We all know the famous *coq au vin*, but why not try it with different poultry and give it a little twist? Guinea fowl has a rich, gamey taste and is wonderful roasted or in a stew such as this one.

Serves 3

Ingredients:
Large knob of butter
2 tsps mild olive oil
1 guinea fowl, jointed
Salt (preferably *fleur de sel*) and fresh pepper
100g lardons
2 shallots, chopped
2 fat garlic cloves, pressed
300ml red wine, preferably a Pinot Noir from Burgundy
100ml port
150ml water
Few sprigs of rosemary, needles finely chopped
250g chestnut mushrooms, quartered
3 tbsps cream

Instructions:

Heat the butter and the oil, and brown the pieces of guinea fowl over a medium-high heat, seasoning them well as you go. Do this in batches and do not crowd the pan! Transfer the browned pieces to a heavy-bottomed casserole. Lower the heat a bit, get rid of some of the fat and cook the lardons, shallots and garlic for approx. 5 minutes. Start adding the liquids bit by bit, stirring as you go. First the wine, then the port, then the water. Pour this sauce over the casserole with the guinea fowl, season with the chopped rosemary and a little more salt and pepper. Bring everything to a brief boil, reduce the heat, cover and allow to simmer for 40 minutes. Add the chestnut mushrooms and allow to cook for an additional 8 minutes with the lid slightly ajar. Remove the guinea fowl from the sauce and add the cream. Let the sauce reduce slightly over a medium-high heat. Serve the guinea fowl with the sauce, a side of mustardy mashed potatoes and the same Pinot Noir used in the stew.

Visiting Autun

The city of Autun has many nice shops, restaurants and cultural attractions. Besides the previously mentioned Roman Amphitheatre and the city's two ancient gateways, the *Musée Rolin*, where one can admire a variety of artifacts, sculptures and beautifully preserved mosaics, is also worth a visit. The museum is housed in the Renaissance hotel built by Nicolas Rolin, also responsible for *L'Hôtel-Dieu* in Beaune. The *Cathédrale St-Lazare*, located on that same square, dates back to the mid-12th century and is famous for its magnificent sculptures and exquisite tympanum executed by Gislebertus, one the best Romanesque sculptors.

There are many good places to eat in Autun, but we always seem to stick to the same place – *Brasserie Le Commerce*. During the afternoons, the brasserie is always filled with the local lunchtime crowd. Always a good sign. If you want to stop by for lunch, it is best to be there before 12:30 in the afternoon as tables are quickly taken, especially in the summer. The dishes served at *Le Commerce* are simple but always wonderful. I've had the creamiest *blanquette de veau* and the most rustic (and stick-to-the-ribs!) *choucroute garnie* in the winter, richly filled seafood salads in the summer, and well, words cannot describe how irresistible their *cocotte de escargots* in garlic sauce truly is!

More than Côte-d'Or: Discovering the great wines of Burgundy's Côte Chalonnaise

To the wine connoisseur, Burgundy is synonymous with the Côte-d'Or. Often referred to as the 'golden slope', the east-facing escarpment produces some of the world's most prestigious wines. Think of big names such as Gevrey-Chambertin and Puligny-Montrachet. These are the giants that have made the region famous. Unfortunately, a bottle bearing such a name on its label is not within everyone's budget. But those who continue farther south, past the town of Chagny, will find the Côte Chalonnaise – a district which is similar to the Côte-d'Or yet produces wines that are significantly more affordable and certainly worth discovering.

Nestled between the Côte de Beaune to the north and the Mâconnais to the south, the Côte Chalonnaise boasts hills of rolling vineyards that intermingle with orchards, meadows and woods. Its vines were planted by the monks of Cluny more than one thousand years ago and today, they stretch out over approximately 25 kilometers and are found at altitudes between 220 and 400 kilometers. The two most important grape varieties produced on the region's clay-limestone soils are Pinot Noir (for red wines) and Chardonnay (for white wines). The exception is the Bouzeron appellation in the north which produces mainly white wines made almost exclusively from the Aligoté grape. A good way to discover the appellations of this relatively underestimated wine district, is to plan a trip that includes panoramic drives through the vineyards, plenty of tastings and a few visits to interesting restaurants.

Bouzeron

Following the *Route des Grands Vins*, your journey through the five main appellations of the Côte Chalonnaise begins in the tiny village of Bouzeron, famous for its pale golden Aligoté wines. These minerally whites with hints of citrus and white flowers are very refreshing, though they might lack fruit and can be slightly acidic. This makes them the perfect choice for a Kir: a local *apéritif* made with Crème de Cassis (see my book *Dishing it Up: The Story behind Twenty Icons of French Food & Drink* for the history of the Kir). Aligoté wines of Bouzeron are best paired with seafood (especially oysters), but they are also delicious with poultry in cream sauce or light salads with goat's cheese. A classic combination is Aligoté paired with the regional speciality of parsleyed ham in aspic known as *jambon persillé*. When visiting Bouzeron, gourmands will want to make a stop at the restaurant Le Bouzeron where Chef Ludovic prepares classic French dishes with the finest seasonal products.

Rully

Heading toward the D981, the next appellation is Rully which produces more whites than reds and has 23 Premiers Crus vineyards. When aged, the crisp, polished whites acquire soft hints of honey and dried fruits. In general, they are lively, well-rounded wines that go exceptionally well with veal and delicate fish dishes. As for the reds, in their youth, they tend to have rather firm tannins which are best balanced by pairing them with creamy dishes such as risottos, offal or rich pastas. Besides its red and white wines, Rully has been the center for sparkling Crémants (an affordable alternative to Champagne) since the 19th century.

But there's more than wine to make your visit to Rully memorable. The majestic Château de Rully which dates back to the 12th century, is perched on a hill overlooking the vineyards and is one of the town's main monuments. It has been owned by the same family since the beginning, and with prior appointment, both visits through the castle and wine tastings can be arranged. Hungry? Many restaurants in the region offer a very reasonably priced *menu du jour* during the afternoon. A great choice is Restaurant Le Vendangerot, where for only 17 euros, you can enjoy a meal that includes cheese or dessert.

Mercurey

Continuing south on the D981, follow the signs to the next appellation – Mercurey. On your way, you'll come across many scenic views where winding roads cut through vineyards and lead to village churches far in the distance. When you enter Mercurey, you will definitely want to make a few stops on *Grande Rue*. This long street is home to various wineries where you can enjoy tastings and talk to passionate growers who have made wine their life's quest. Two highly recommended choices are Domaine Michel Juillot and Le Clos Antonin Rodet. The Caveau Divin Mercurey, where 35 estates are collectively represented, is also worth a visit.

Mercurey is the most important appellation by far and has 32 Premiers Crus vineyards spread over roughly 650 hectares. It is the district's largest volume producer, and in fact, the Côte Chalonnaise was once called the 'Région de Mercurey.' The appellation is predominantly known for its deep ruby reds, which when aged, develop hints of cocoa and tobacco. Keep them for five to eight years and enjoy the rich, fleshy wines with Charolais steaks, duck confit and potato gratins.

Givry

Just a few kilometers farther on, is the small village of Givry, which together with Dracy-le-Fort and Jambles, is home to 26 Premiers Crus vineyards. The appellation produces balanced whites but is mostly known for its reds. In their youth, the reds tend to be quite tannic, so it is best to keep them for a minimum of three to five years before opening. Red Givry wines are a fine choice for terrines and pâtés, but they are also wonderful served with the region's Bresse poultry or strong cheeses. During your visit to Givry, sights not to be missed include the *Hôtel de Ville* (one of France's most beautiful town halls built in the second half of the 18th century as a monumental port) and *La Halle Ronde* (a circular grain market situated in the center of town and dating to 1825-1830).

Montagny

The final destination of a wine journey through the Côte Chalonnaise is Montagny. The appellation spans four villages: Montagny, Buxy, Saint-Vallerin and Jully-lès-Buxy. White wines are solely produced in Montagny, and the appellation has the highest concentration of Premiers Crus vineyards – namely, 49. The whites are delicately floral, fresh, and with their brilliance, perfect partners for aromatic dishes such as fish tagines, paella or Asian fare. Well worth a visit is the friendly village of Buxy which has a superb restaurant (Aux Années Vins), a winemaker's museum where you can learn more about wine production and a cooperative cellar offering fine selections of the region's wines. Although the Côte Chalonnaise does not boast any Grand Cru appellations or enjoy the prestige of the Côte-d'Or, its wines do not disappoint. From Bouzeron to Montagny, and whether it be wine, gastronomy or simply enjoying the unspoilt French countryside, the Côte Chalonnaise delights the senses in a multitude of ways. If you can, I highly recommend you plan a little gourmet getaway to one of France's most beautiful (and affordable) wine-producing regions.

The mysterious lake (Diary entry)

The weather was absolutely gorgeous today. After breakfast, we stopped by the butcher in Buxy where we purchased two Charolais *entrecôtes* for us and a tomato-mushroom Charolais burger for Kirstie. With some garlicky *pommes sarladaises* and a bottle of Mercurey, that would be dinner that evening.

The plan was to go in search of a small lake for Kirstie to swim in. There was only one in the village, we had been told, and it was obviously well hidden from tourists like us. The local secret perhaps? Determined to find it, we walked through fields of tall grass, pretty flowers, all sorts of wildly buzzing insects and peacefully grazing cows. Unfortunately, our adventurous journey only led to a small puddle of water, and after walking for what seemed like hours, we decided to make our way back home before the afternoon heat would set in. She had been looking forward to a good swim and was very disappointed. Luckily, baguette sandwiches with *jambon du morvan* can cure many ails.

Chicken in Banyuls

How I love French markets like the one in Chalon-sur-Saône. Stall after stall of beautiful, fresh produce; cheeses; meats and *charcuterie*; wines; fresh herbs and dried exotic spices; the best fruits and vegetables; succulent, tasty olives; and beautiful dried sausages in every flavor imaginable! Everyone is in a good mood. Some people are trying a piece of sweet melon, others a fragrant little olive. Many are engaged in conversation with the vendors, while some are watching the spectacle from one of the many restaurants and bars in front of the church.

Le Verre Galant in Chalon-sur-Saône, a restaurant/wine bar we keep coming back to, is situated on the market square. The owner is very friendly, and the *formule du jour* (which includes wine, dessert and coffee) is always delicious and satisfying. In the warmer months, we have our meal outdoors. It's lovely to order a drink and wait for our meal while watching the hustle and bustle of the market.

I am always inspired by the simple, French dishes

they serve at this restaurant. The last time we ate there we had a dish of duckling in Banyuls, a sweet fortified wine from the coastal town of Banyuls-sur-Mer. It is somewhat similar to Port and is wonderful served with dessert. But oh my was it fantastic with duckling!

I tried recreating this dish with chicken quarters instead of duckling. This time, I dare say that my version was even a little better than the one I had at the restaurant.

Serve this aromatic chicken dish with mashed potatoes or steamed rice and a side of seasonal vegetables. In summer, I like to serve this with parsleyed courgettes.

Serves 3

Ingredients:
3 chicken quarters
350ml Banyuls
3 garlic cloves, pressed
1 sprig of rosemary, needles finely chopped
Salt (preferably *fleur de sel*) and fresh pepper
1 tsp fine Dijon mustard
1 tbsp honey
Olive oil

Instructions:
Put the chicken quarters in a casserole. Whisk the Banyuls, garlic, rosemary, salt, pepper, mustard and honey. Pour over the chicken and allow it to

marinate for at least 3 hours. When ready to cook the chicken, take it out of the marinade, pat it dry and brown it in a little olive oil. Pour the marinade over the browned chicken, cover and cook for 45 minutes to 1 hour. If the sauce thickens too much toward the end of the cooking time, add a little water.

Nose-to-tail

While I do enjoy a piece of fried blood sausage (*boudin noir*) and can admit that as a child, one of my favorite treats was a steamy bowl of tripe soup, I still have a lot to discover.

I have great admiration for people who are fearless when it comes to eating every part of an animal, like my late uncle who told us about the joys of fried bull's testicles with scrambled eggs. It was a favorite breakfast dish, and he hated that testicles weren't as readily available as they were while he was growing up. My father adores stewed tongue. It is the dish he requests on birthdays and other special occasions. Tongue is as much a treat to him as a bottle of fine wine is to me. *But oh that smell!* Sour, pungent and thick enough to stick around the house long after the meal was cooked and eaten. Disgusting you say? Not at all! Why call something 'disgusting' before we've even had the chance to try it? And is there really anything disgusting about using up every last bit of the animals we slaughter for food?

Much to my admiration, the French pretty much

share this same philosophy. Just walk around a market in France or have a good look at the meat section at a supermarket, and you'll see what I mean. They're not picky. Everything is eaten. Take *andouillette*, for example, a food that many foreigners fear. Some, who have naively ordered *andouillette* at a restaurant, recall the traumatizing experience of cutting into what seemed like an ordinary sausage and nearly fainting from the odor. Not surprising, since the sausage's main ingredient is chitterlings, or pork intestines. While it's true that *andouillette* doesn't exactly smell like freshly baked apple pie, (it's often described as 'very offensive' and said to 'genuinely stink of shit'), to many French, *andouillette* is considered one of the most beloved *charcuteries*. Authentic *cuisine du terroir*. And who are we to think we know better? What if we're the ones missing out?

I can't help but wonder why and when we all suddenly developed such picky eating habits. Why is one part of the animal better than the other or more acceptable to eat? Nobody blinks an eye when someone eats chicken breast, but if you happen to enjoy a soup made with its feet! And why do people who repulse at the horrors of *foie gras* still hop on over to their local supermarket to stock up on ridiculously cheap trays of industrial meat? Talk about horror!

Perhaps it's time to reconsider our eating habits. Let's try to think out of the box and remember that there's more to life than chicken breast and meatballs. I might just walk up to my butcher sometime in the near future and order half a pig's head and a couple of trotters. It's never too late to try my hand at making *fromage de tête* – I hear it's a lovely starter.

Bon appétit!

Chapter 3

France On Your Plate

Summer Outdoor Feasts

The summer is the perfect time to get out and enjoy the outdoors. Why not take your picnic basket to a quiet spot under a shady tree, listen to the birds sing and feel the grass between your toes? Or have dinner outside at a beautifully decorated table set with pretty tea lights, antique plates and your best silverware?

The following recipes demand to be enjoyed on warm summer days. The salad makes a perfect light lunch, the chicken is great for a sultry summer evening's barbecue, and the ice cream – well, you'll just have to try the ice cream!

Salade d'été

During the warmer months, salads are not only healthy but also deliciously refreshing. Get inspired by nature and use fresh ingredients for more variations in taste, color and texture. Served with bread and paired with a good wine, summer salads make a perfect light meal. Pure, fresh and bursting with vitamins!

This salad is truly summer on a plate: crunchy walnuts, crusty bread topped with a creamy layer of grilled goat's cheese, thin slices of raw ham, and as a finishing touch, sunny raspberries that shine like edible jewels between the salad greens.

The salad makes a wonderful, light lunch for two, but you can also offer it as an elegant starter for four. If you serve the salad as a starter to a barbecue, follow it with a grilled leg of lamb and round off the meal with a creamy dessert such a *crème brulée* dusted with a touch of lavender sugar.

Serves 2 as a light lunch or 4 as a starter

Ingredients:
For the dressing:

1 tbsp Dijon mustard
3 tbsps walnut oil
1 tbsp sherry vinegar
2 tsps honey
Salt (preferably *fleur de sel*) and fresh pepper

For the salad:
50g walnuts, roughly chopped
2 slices *pain de campagne*
4 petits *chèvre doux* (soft goat's cheese)
100g mixed baby leaves
100g fresh raspberries
6 slices raw ham

Instructions:

Whisk all the ingredients for the dressing in a large bowl until they emulsify. Roast the walnuts in an ungreased frying pan until they release their delicious aroma. This usually takes 2-3 minutes. Spread the goat's cheese on the slices of bread and place them under a hot grill until the cheese begins to bubble and brown in some places. Place the baby leaves in the bowl with the dressing and toss to coat. Divide the salad between two plates and sprinkle with the walnuts. Top with the fresh raspberries and ham. Cut each warm slice of bread in half and place both halves on top of the salad. Serve immediately, preferably with a lively, aromatic Sancerre.

Poulet en crapaudine

Making *poulet en crapaudine* may seem difficult, but it certainly isn't. The only thing you have to do is butterfly the chicken by removing the backbone and pressing firmly on its breast so that it lies as flat as possible. If you don't have a pair of heavy-duty kitchen shears, this will probably be a job you'll want to leave to your butcher. The chicken gets its tenderness and warm, rich flavor from a marinade of fresh herbs, garlic and lots of lemon juice. *Poulet en crapaudine* is great on the barbecue served in combination with grilled green asparagus, crusty bread and an oaky, fleshy Chardonnay.

Note: Save the backbone for stock.

Serves 4

Ingredients:
1 whole chicken
A large, Ziploc bag
1 organic lemon, sliced
1 tsp salt (preferably *fleur de sel*)
2 tsps pink peppercorns

Small bunch of thyme
Small bunch of rosemary
3 cloves pink garlic (*ail rose*), thinly sliced

Instructions:

Place the chicken on a large platter, breast side down and feel for its backbone. Use heavy-duty shears to cut down one side of the backbone and then down the other side. Turn the chicken over and press firmly on its breast and legs so that it lies as flat as possible. Put the chicken in a Ziploc bag and add all the ingredients. Zip the bag closed and massage the ingredients into the chicken. Allow the chicken to marinate in the fridge for 2-3 hours, remembering to take it out of the fridge half an hour before grilling it. Grill the chicken for approx. 1 hour, turning it frequently. You can check if the chicken is ready by making a small incision between the leg and the breast. If the juices run clear (no longer pink), the chicken is done.

Salted caramel ice cream

We all know and (most of us) love salted caramel, and I am no exception. I've made this ice cream for dinner parties and my guests always rave about it, asking me to send them the recipe as they wave goodbye at the end of the night. Because the flavor is quite intense, and because good things come in small sizes, I suggest that you serve the ice cream in tiny espresso cups.

Note: Making caramel really isn't all that difficult. The most important thing to remember is that you should not (never ever!) stir when heating the sugar. Just swirl the mixture ever so gently as the sugar begins to caramelize. Immediately take the pan off the heat as soon as the sugar turns the color of maple syrup.
Please, please, please be very careful when making caramel and make sure that children and pets are far away from the kitchen. Hot caramel causes horrible burns!!

Serves 10

Ingredients:
180g fine sugar
50g butter
250ml cream
1 tsp *fleur de sel*
350ml whole milk
4 egg yolks

Instructions:
Put the sugar in a pan over medium heat and wait until it starts to caramelize. At that point, you can gently shake the pan. Once the sugar caramelizes and becomes the color of maple syrup, take it off of the heat. Add the butter, cream and salt and stir carefully but vigorously with a whisk. The caramel will stick to the whisk, and that's fine. Put the pan back on the stove over a medium heat and whisk until the caramel is dissolved. Add the milk and whisk again. Beat the egg yolks with the vanilla extract and whisk them into the milk-caramel mixture. Whisk vigorously! Otherwise, the eggs will curdle. Allow the custard to cook on a very gentle heat for approx. 15 minutes, stirring occasionally. The custard should be thick enough to coat the back of a spoon. Pour the custard into a bowl, allow it to cool and then refrigerate for 2 hours. Churn the ice cream in an ice cream machine. Take the ice cream out of the freezer 5 minutes before serving so that it softens.

Asparagus & capers tart

The combination of goat's cheese, capers and the season's best green asparagus is simply divine. Serve this tart as a light starter or lunch with a crisp Sauvignon Blanc or a Riesling.

Serves 4 as a light lunch and 8 as a starter

Ingredients:
400g thin green asparagus, ends trimmed
Rectangular sheet of ready-made puff pastry
200ml *crème fraîche*
100g soft, spreadable goat's cheese
2 tbsps capers
Salt (preferably *fleur de sel*) and fresh pepper
A little milk, for brushing

Instructions:
Preheat the oven to 200°C. Roll out the puff pastry and place it on a baking sheet lined with baking paper. Boil the asparagus for 3-5 minutes, drain and rinse quickly with cold water. Place them on a clean dish cloth. Whisk the *crème fraîche*, goat's cheese, capers and salt and pepper. Don't use too

much salt as the capers are quite salty! Spread the mixture evenly over the pastry leaving an edge free all around. Top with the asparagus. Brush a little milk on the edges of the pastry and bake for approx. 30 minutes.

Marché Victor Hugo: An epicurean dream

Toulouse, the 'Pink City' located on the banks of the Garonne River, is the fourth largest city in France and a food lover's paradise boasting a variety of wonderful restaurants, exceptional regional specialities and vibrant food markets.
One of those markets is Marché Victor Hugo. Although its location is anything but glamorous (the stalls are located on the ground floor of a 1970s car park building), the food reflects why Toulouse is an epicenter of authentic French cuisine. More than one hundred passionate vendors gather at *Place Victor Hugo* every morning from Tuesday to Sunday to offer the public an impressive choice of local products, the freshest seafood, breads, pastries, wine and just about every type of cheese imaginable. Early in the day, before curious tourists arrive, it is the locals who are rushing about with their empty wicker baskets or trolleys, which soon enough are filled with food that looks like it came straight out of a Baroque painting.

I found the market by chance on a cloudy July morning. From the opposite side of the street, I noticed the stalls with crates filled with a rainbow of seasonal fruits and vegetables, and I remember thinking how this sumptuous display seemed to add a much-needed shot of color to what looked like the start of an unseasonably dreary summer day. As I came a little closer, I had a lesson in the art of buying fresh produce, which obviously involves probing, sniffing and poking. This was more than your average shopping for the sheer sake of sustenance. It was serious business in the name of the pleasures of the palate. And the inside of this culinary paradise was even more tempting than the outside.

To start, the meat: nothing short of a carnivore's naughtiest fantasy. Butchers offering marbled cuts of beef, thick slabs of pork, elegant racks of lamb, whole unskinned rabbits, poultry complete with head and claws, legs of preserved duck covered in their own fat, and of course, huge coils of the gleaming *Saucisse de Toulouse* made with coarsely ground pork. And because the nose-to-tail philosophy is so deeply rooted in French cuisine, pork's trotters and heads, whole beef tongues, tripe, brains, hearts and other kinds of offal were also prominently displayed. Unusual to some, but here, nothing out of the ordinary. I was especially in awe of the stunning assortment of charcuterie: all varieties of dried sausages flavored with herbs and spices, cured hams, unctuous rillettes, rustic pâtés and tins of foie gras. There were jars of *cassoulet* (a thick, hearty stew, see note), so that sampling the rustic regional dish would need no more than a bit of reheating.

Seafood stalls were arranged in exuberant mounds of delight with live crabs, langoustines and lobsters, whole fish, sumptuous king-sized shrimp and baskets brimming with beautiful oysters.

And then everything from pasta to pastries and even wines. I didn't want to wake up from this epicurean dream...

Note: *Cassoulet* is a creamy bean and meat stew blanketed by an irresistibly crisp, golden crust. It is the epitome of comfort food. First mentioned in a *Le Viandier*, a recipe collection dating to the 14th century, the origins of the emblematic dish have been the source of much debate. Three places have claimed it as their own: the beautifully preserved, fortified city of Carcassonne, one of Occitanie's eight UNESCO World Heritage Sites; Toulouse; and Castelnaudary, located halfway between the two. Castelnaudary, however, was acknowledged as the capital of *cassoulet* by Parisian chef and culinary writer Prosper Montagné in his book, *Le Festin Occitan* (1929). He not only propelled the dish to worldwide fame, but also struck a truce between the three cities when he declared that: "*Cassoulet* is the God of Occitan cuisine. One God in three persons: God the father is the *cassoulet* of Castelnaudary, God the son is that of Carcassonne, and the Holy Spirit that of Toulouse."

Soupe froide de courgettes

One of the quieter *bastides** in Lot-et-Garonne is Miramont-de-Guyenne, founded by English King Edward I in 1278. Though there aren't many major attractions, it's a joy to stroll through the town's sleepy streets, stopping along the way to admire its two churches: the 13th-century *Église de Beffrey* and the *Église Sainte-Marie* dating to 1860.

At *midi*, we are always one of the first to grab a table at Bistrot du Commerce, situated directly in front of the *mairie* on *Place de l'Hôtel de Ville*. It's the perfect place to experience what a French two-hour lunch break really is. This friendly eatery serves a consistently delicious three-course menu which is a hit with local office workers who will not hesitate to start their meal with an *apéritif* or wash it down with a glass of wine!

During one of the rare Dutch heatwaves, as I struggled to find the energy to cook, I suddenly remembered a soup I had as a starter to a three-course lunch at this lovely restaurant. After a walk around the village, this chilled, minty soup was the ultimate refreshment and a great start to a wonderful summer meal.

* Bastides or 'new towns' (*villes nouvelles*) were established by French and English rulers between 1152 and 1453 in order to assert authority, bring structure to the expanding population and encourage trade in Lot-et-Garonne.

Serves 4

Ingredients:
2 tbsps olive oil, plus extra to serve
1 shallot, thinly sliced
4 baby courgettes (approx. 450g), sliced
Salt (preferably *fleur de sel*)
500ml vegetable bouillon
3 garlic cloves, sliced
Small bunch of mint, leaves picked
50ml cream

Instructions:
Heat the oil in a heavy-bottomed soup pan and gently sauté the shallots for 4 minutes. Add the baby courgettes and salt and cook for 4 minutes. Pour in the stock, bring to the boil, reduce the heat and simmer for 6 minutes. Add the garlic and cook for an additional 2 minutes. Take the pan off the heat and cool in a sink full of cold water. Once cooled, add the mint and cream and purée with a handheld mixer or in a blender. Transfer to a glass jug or bottle and refrigerate. Enjoy chilled with a drizzle of olive oil.

Roast chicken & chickpea salad

Approximately 20km to the northwest of Miramont-de-Guyenne is Duras, an endearing village overlooking the Dropt Valley and known for its imposing 12th-century château. Duras attracts wine lovers with an appellation that has produced exceptional quality (and very affordable!) wines since the 12th century. Stretching out over 1524 hectares, the Côtes de Duras is part of the Bergerac wine region and counts some 200 dedicated winegrowers who make everything from bold reds to sweet dessert wines.

Duras has a warmth that captivated us from the very first time we visited. We love its history, people, friendly restaurants and cafés, and neighboring villages. It is a beautiful little corner of the world that has stolen our hearts without. I came up with this easy salad recipe after buying a roast chicken at the market in Duras one Monday morning. They are always so hard to resist. You'll see them slowly roasting on a spit, and with each turn, becoming more succulent and golden than ever. That afternoon, we ate half of the chicken with a side of potatoes (roasted directly under the birds). Here's what I did with the leftovers. You won't need much to serve with this, except a smooth glass of red wine from Duras, of course.

Serves 4

Ingredients:
½ a roast chicken
2 cans of chickpeas (400g each)
1 bunch of flat-leaf parsley, chopped
3 spring onions, chopped
5 tbsps capers
200g cherry tomatoes, halved or quartered, depending on their size
Juice of half a lemon
50ml extra virgin olive oil
Salt (preferably *fleur de sel*) and fresh pepper

Instructions:
Pluck the meat from the roast chicken and put it in a large bowl. Rinse the chickpeas in a colander under cold running water and drain well. Put them in the bowl with the chicken. Add the parsley, spring onions, capers and cherry tomatoes. Make a dressing by whisking the lemon juice with the olive oil and salt and pepper. Pour the dressing over the ingredients in the bowl and stir carefully to combine. Serve, savor and swoon!

Lime panna cotta with roasted apricots

One of my favorite restaurants in Duras is La Terrasse, situated directly in front of the *château* and run by the friendly couple Mathias and Eléonore Billaud. The *à la carte* menu features regional classics such as *confit de canard* and silky *foie gras* as well as juicy steaks, a few seafood options and even an excellent fish n' chips, always popular with the village's large English expat population and tourists.

La Terrasse also serves an excellent three-course set menu on weekdays with creative dishes that always inspire me. Like the panna cotta that was so good, I had to immediately pause after the first bite to make notes on my phone. This version is quite different from the one I enjoyed that afternoon, but extremely delicious nonetheless.

Serves 4

Ingredients
200g cream

½ vanilla pod, seeds scraped out
3 tbsps honey
5 gelatine leaves
Zest of 1 organic lime & juice of 3 limes
200ml whole yogurt

For the apricots:
4 apricots, halved
Juice & zest of 1 organic lime
1 tbsp honey
60ml water

Instructions:

Place the cream, vanilla seeds (and pod), lime zest and honey in a small saucepan and gently heat without boiling. Whisk occasionally. In the meantime, soak the gelatine leaves in cold water. Whisk the yogurt with the lime juice. Remove the gelatine leaves from the water, squeezing them out thoroughly, and add to the hot cream mixture. Whisk until dissolved. Whisk in the yogurt. Lightly oil 4 ramekins and divide the mixture over them evenly. Allow to set in the fridge for at least 5 hours. For the apricots, preheat the oven to 180°C. Place the apricots cut side up on a small baking dish. Top with the zest, honey, juice and water. Bake for 18 minutes and allow to cool thoroughly before refrigerating. To release the panna cottas, gently place them in a baking dish filled with hot water for approx. 20 seconds. They should now slip out easily, but you can give them a little help by running the tip of a small knife around the edges. Serve the panna cotta with the roasted apricots.

Memorable meal in Duras

One of the most memorable meals I have ever been invited to took place years ago in Duras; a barbecue hosted by a lovely family we had met there.

We were expected for the *apéritif* at seven in the evening. The weather had been somewhat cloudy that day so there was definitely a chance that we would have to postpone our plans. Luckily, by the time we had to leave, the dark clouds cleared and we arrived at Tessa and Jean-Claude's doorstep, wine and chocolates in hand, and very much looking forward to an evening of outdoor dining *à la campagne*.

We took a seat at the large wooden table in the garden as Tessa brought out some crackers and nuts for us to munch on with our Pastis. While she darted back and forth between the kitchen and garden, we engaged in conversation with the chatty Jean-Claude who told us that he had just built the terrace we were sitting at and about all his other future building plans. The children happily frolicked about, grabbing some nuts here and there and asking when dinner would be ready. I remember feeling very lucky that evening. I had always secretly hoped to be invited to dinner with a family in France, and I knew this meal was going to be great, even before Tessa had a chance to delight us with her culinary skills.

Dinner started with a board of sliced *pâté* accompanied by tiny, sweet cornichons and a small jar of onion confit, perhaps the most perfect of accompaniments to any charcuterie. I was given a knife and instructed to cut rounds from a crusty baguette. In the meantime, Jean-Claude opened a bottle of the local Sauvignon Blanc. The night was young and the conversation was as light as our spirits as we toasted to the good life and good food.

The next course was a bright courgette soup, creamy yet light enough to let the flavor of the summer courgettes shine through. Tessa served it in colorful shallow bowls and garnished each portion with a vivid orange nasturtium blossom. We laughed and made jokes as she told us how to suck out the nectar from the stem. The soup was so exquisite and delicate that we almost forgot that we had actually been invited to a barbecue. A six-course, very French barbecue!

After the soup, Jean-Claude busied himself grilling an assortment of delicately marinated skewered meats, and in the meantime, Tessa set out bowls of bean and pasta salads. We joyfully ate, washing down our meal with glasses that were never allowed to go empty, and when the skies grew darker, we lit candles and talked about pursuing dreams, about letting go of fears and about taking risks. At that moment, the sultry evening air, my beloved France, the good company and the gorgeous food was pure, sheer bliss.

When the cheese platter came out, Jean-Claude and I discussed our appreciation for stinky cheeses, snails and other French delicacies. Dessert was a perfect (and very refreshing) culmination to a lovely evening. We enjoyed sunny, orange slices of Charentais melon. Like the courgette soup, the melon was a delicious reflection of the summer's bounty. Tessa told us that she had shopped for most of the products at the market that morning and that some came from a village farmer.

I will always have fond memories of that evening. While being served seared foie gras on brioche might impress me, I am more in awe of people like Tessa and Jean-Claude, people who are obviously passionate about food, but mostly, about life. That meal was more than a barbecue. It was a feast prepared with love. Love for the food and for the enjoyment that comes with eating it in good company.

Courgette soup with mascarpone & pesto

A velvety soup full of bright summer flavors and inspired by the one Tessa made for us that evening. Serve it with garlic toasted topped with chopped tomatoes and fragrant basil.

Serves 4

Ingredients:
2 tbsps olive oil
1 shallot, finely chopped
1 garlic clove, finely chopped
3 courgettes (or 6 small baby courgettes), cubed
450ml vegetable bouillon
125ml dry white wine
3 tbsps mascarpone
2 tbsps pesto
Salt (preferably *fleur de sel*) and fresh pepper

Instructions:
Heat the oil in a heavy-bottomed pan and gently cook the onions and the garlic for approx. 5

minutes. Increase the heat and add the courgettes. Allow the courgettes to cook, tossing them as you go, for approx. 2-3 minutes. Add the wine and let it bubble for about a minute. Add the water, bouillon, and salt and pepper to taste. Let everything come to the boil and immediately reduce the heat. Cover the pan and let the soup simmer for 20 minutes. Remove the pan from the heat and stir in the mascarpone and the pesto until well incorporated. Purée the soup in a blender or with a handheld mixer, taste, adjust the seasoning and serve.

Tartelettes aux fraises

These pretty strawberry tartelettes do require a bit of effort, but it is well worth it. They look and taste like they came straight out of a French bakery!

Note: You will need 10cm molds.
These tartelettes are delicious with just about any fruit. Try them with raspberries or sweet, juicy peaches!

Makes 4

Ingredients:
For the crème pâtissière:
200 ml whole milk
2 egg yolks
65g sugar
½ tsp vanilla extract
Pinch of salt (preferably fleur de sel)
1 ½ all-purpose tbsps flour

Instructions:
Make this at least a few hours in advance as you want it nice and cold. Heat the milk, taking care

not to let it boil. In a large bowl, whisk the egg yolks, sugar, vanilla extract and salt until creamy. Preferably, do this by hand as you don't want too much volume in the mixture. Whisk in the flour. Start adding the milk in small quantities while vigorously whisking. Transfer the mixture to a pan and cook it while stirring continuously with a wooden spoon. Do not walk away from the stove and do not stop stirring. Cook for 3-5 minutes until the pastry cream is nice and thick. Allow to cool and refrigerate.

Ingredients:
For the tartelette cases:
150g all-purpose flour
75g cold butter, cubed
2 tbsps fine sugar
1 egg
Pinch of salt (preferably *fleur de sel*)

Instructions:
Place all the ingredients in your food processor and pulse until the dough comes together in a ball. Shape into a disk and refrigerate for at least 1 hour. After that, preheat your oven to 190°C and roll out your dough to a thickness of about 3mm. Place the tartelette molds upside down on the dough and cut a circle around them, slightly bigger than their actual circumference. Grease the molds with butter and dust them with flour, shaking off any excess. Press the dough into the molds and prick their

surface with a fork. Place a sheet of baking paper on each mold and weigh down with baking beans. Bake the cases for 20-25 minutes, remove from their molds and allow to cool.

To assemble the tartelettes:

Ingredients:
1 tbsp strawberry jam
¾ tbsp water
225g strawberries

Instructions:
Once the tartelettes shells are completely cool, put the jam and the water in a pan and whisk over medium heat for a minute or so. This will be the glaze for the berries. To assemble the tarts, divide the pastry cream over the shells, top with halved strawberries and brush with the glaze.

The French apéro

L'heure de l'apéro is a small luxury we should all make room for in our lives. Imagine the pleasure of coming home from work and enjoying a drink (*apéritif*) and nibble instead of hurrying to cook and get dinner on the table. This most delightful of French food and drink rituals is the ultimate way to leave the stresses of the day behind and prepare for a relaxed evening meal. While I do understand this is hardly practical on a daily basis, it is something to keep in mind on Friday evenings or when welcoming dinner guests to your home.

Keep in mind that the drinks offered should not be too heavy as to spoil the appetite. Kir (white wine mixed with crème de cassis, crème de pêche or crème de framboise), Port, Vermouth, sparkling drinks such as Crémant or Champagne, Campari, Pastis, Lillet, Suze or even a gin-tonic are all great choices. If serving wine as an *apéritif*, opt for white wine, rosé or even a sweet wine. Red wine is much too strong, in my opinion. Typical foods served with an *apéritif* are olives, bread and rillettes, artisanal sausages or other charcuterie, a chunk of pâté with a few cornichons, and even some quality chips. None of them, obviously, involve any cooking. A stop at a delicatessen on your way home from work should suffice.

If, however, you want to add your own little touch to your *apéro*, or if you would like to host an *apéritif dînatoire* for friends – which is meant as a meal and similar to a buffet – the following recipes are easy to make and incredibly delicious.

Tuna rillettes with ras el hanout

Though my favorite rillettes are made from pork or duck, I also enjoy making rillettes with canned fish and serving it on melba toasts as part of an *apéro*. Serve with a chilled Sauvignon Blanc.

Makes approx. 100g

Ingredients:
Can of tuna in water (160g), drained
1 tsp ras el hanout
2 tsps capers
1 tbsp mayonnaise
¼ shallot, chopped
1 garlic clove, chopped
Few drops of lemon juice
Fresh pepper
Chili powder & finely chopped chives, to garnish

Instructions:
Place all the ingredients (except the chili powder and chives) in a small kitchen machine and process till smooth. Transfer to a jar or bowl and garnish with the chili and chives.

Cake salé with baby courgettes, chèvre & green olives

Delicious cubed as part of an *apéro* or with soup (for lunch). Also lovely with a green salad and a mustardy vinaigrette.

Makes 1 cake

Ingredients:
140g all-purpose flour
60g whole-wheat flour
1 tbsp baking powder
1 tbsp dried basil
Fresh pepper
3 eggs
150ml white wine
4 tbsps olive oil
50g chèvre, in small pieces
2 baby courgette s(approx. 150g)
50g green olives, chopped

Instructions:
Preheat the oven to 180°C and line a 26 x 11cm

cake pan with baking paper. In a large bowl, mix the two flours, baking powder, dried basil and pepper. In a jug, whisk eggs, wine and oil. Add the wet ingredients to the dry and gently mix with a spatula. Add the chèvre, baby courgettes and olives and gently fold into the batter. Pour the batter into the prepared cake pan and bake for approx. 40-45 minutes. Allow to cool before serving.

Pink garlic from Lautrec

I cannot possibly leave France without bringing back a beautiful, sturdy bunch of pink garlic (called a *'manouille'* in French) as an edible souvenir. From the very first time I tried *Ail Rose de Lautrec*, I fell in love with its distinctive flavor. Normal garlic is just plain boring and much too sharp, masking and often overpowering the taste of food, rather than subtly enhancing it.

The story of pink garlic begins in the Middle Ages when it was first used in the Tarn department. During the 19th century, it was produced in small quantities and sold at the local markets of Mazamet, Castres and Albi, but it wasn't until the 1950s, however, that the cultivation of pink garlic really took off. In 1959, small-scale producers established the *Syndicat de Défense du Label Rouge Ail Rose de Lautrec*. By 1966, pink garlic had obtained the *Label Rouge* certification guaranteeing optimum quality ensured by stringent production methods. Three decades later it received the *Indication Géographique Protégée* (IGP) label. Today there are 360 hectares producing between four hundred and eight hundred tons of pink garlic every year in Tarn. The garlic is planted in December and January and harvested at the end of June. After that, it is allowed a minimum drying time of two weeks before the roots are removed and the garlic is peeled down to the last layer of skin. The final step involves the calibration of the garlic and the packaging or tying into its signature bunches.

If stored in a dry, well-ventilated area with a temperature between 12°C to 15 °C, the garlic will remain firm and fragrant for at least six months and up to a year. On the first Friday and Saturday in August, Lautrec holds its annual pink garlic festival with all kinds of activities, music and plenty of tastings. If you ever get the chance to visit, the pink garlic soup is a must!

Pink garlic cream soup
A very simple and garlicky soup. Wonderful in the late summer, but perfect in the winter when you're feeling a little under the weather.
Serves 4- 6

Ingredients:
1 ½L vegetable bouillon
175ml cream
10 pink garlic cloves, pressed
Finely chopped flat-leaf parsley, to serve

Instructions:

Bring the bouillon to the boil and add the pink garlic. Turn the heat down to a simmer and allow the soup to cook gently for 8 minutes. Add the cream, whisking it in thoroughly. Allow the soup to simmer for another minute or two, whisk again and serve immediately with the chopped parsley.

Sardines with lemon & piment d'Espelette

Sardines are not only healthy and inexpensive, but also very delicious. Serve them with a salad or tomates à la Provençale (see the recipe in my book *Market Fresh Cooking*).

Serves 2

Ingredients:
4 medium sardines (whole)
Olive oil
Zest and juice of ½ organic lemon
1 ½ tsps *piment d'Espelette*
Salt (preferably *fleur de sel*)
2 garlic cloves, sliced
Flat-leaf parsley, chopped

Instructions:
Clean the sardines (remove scales, heads, entrails and spine, then rinse well and pat dry). Place the sardines on a plate skin-side up and season with olive oil, lemon zest, *piment d'Espelette* and salt. Heat approx. 3 tbsps olive oil in a large nonstick

fish pan or skillet and add the sardines skin-side down. Season the other side with *piment d'Espelette* and salt. Cook the sardines for approx. 2-3 minutes a side. Add the garlic and lemon juice toward the end of the cooking time. Serve the sardines with a scattering of parsley.

Tomato tarte tatin

Savory variations of sweet recipes always arouse my curiosity. Like a salted cake for an *apéro* instead of tea. A clafoutis with cheese and broccoli instead of cherries or other fruit. *Madeleines* with ham, chives and cheddar. A *crème brulée* with goat's cheese. Or a *tarte tatin* with tomatoes instead of apples.
This recipe screams summer and makes a beautiful lunch when tomatoes are abundant and at their ripest and most fragrant. Though you can use ready-made pastry, my recipe is done in a flash.

Note: Preferably, the *tarte tatin* should be made in an authentic *tarte tatin* pan measuring 25cm. One that can also be used on the stove. You can also use an ovenproof pan of the same size.

Serves 4

Ingredients:
For the pastry:
250g flour
Pinch of salt (preferably *fleur de sel*)
110g cold butter, cubed

40g cold margarine, cubed
1 egg
2 tsps cold water

For the filling:
2 tbsps olive oil
700g ripe plum tomatoes, halved
Salt (preferably *fleur de sel*) and fresh pepper
3 garlic cloves, sliced

Instructions:

In the bowl of your food processor, pulse the flour, salt, butter and margarine until the mixture resembles coarse breadcrumbs. Then add the egg and the water, and pulse again until the dough comes together. On a well-floured surface, roll out the pastry to a circle that is slightly larger than the pan you will be using. Put the pastry circle in the fridge to chill for at least 1 hour. Preheat the oven to 180°C. Put the pan on the stove and heat the oil. Add the tomatoes face up and season with salt and pepper. Cook for 4 minutes, turning them over frequently and seasoning the other side. Make sure the tomatoes are facing up when you are ready to transfer them to the oven. Bake for 20 minutes. Take the pastry out of the fridge 10 minutes before the end of the baking time. Once the tomatoes are cooked, take the pan out of the oven. You will notice the tomatoes have released a lot of juices, and this is perfectly fine. Scatter the tomatoes with the garlic and carefully cover with the pastry making sure to tuck it into the sides. Prick the pastry a few times with the tip of a knife. Bake the *tarte tatin* for approx. 45 minutes. To serve, place a large plate on top of the pan, put on some oven gloves, and flip the whole thing over so that the *tarte tatin* ends up on your plate. Delicious with a green salad.

Radish greens soup

The next time you buy fresh radishes at the market, do not discard the greens! They are wonderful in this nutritious soup. Just make sure you use organic radishes that haven't been sprayed with pesticides.

Serves 4

Ingredients:
1 knob of butter
1 tbsp olive oil
1 large onion, finely chopped
200g potatoes, chopped
3 garlic cloves, chopped
650ml vegetable stock
Bunch of radish tops, washed well
Salt (preferably *fleur de sel*) & fresh pepper
100ml cream

Instructions:
Heat the butter and olive oil in a heavy-bottomed soup pan and gently sauté the onion for approx. 4 minutes. Add the potatoes and garlic and cook for an additional 5 minutes. Add the stock, bring

everything to a boil, reduce the heat and stir in the radish greens. Season with salt and pepper. Simmer for 15 minutes with a lid on. Add the cream and purée the soup with a handheld mixer. Taste, adjust the seasoning if necessary and serve with a fresh grinding of pepper and a swirl of olive oil.

Rhubarb & vanilla cake

Keep this easy recipe in mind when rhubarb is in season. It's delightful with a good drizzle of *crème anglaise*, just like I enjoyed it at a *salon de thé* in the lovely village of Eymet in Dordogne years ago.

Serves 6

Ingredients:
150g rhubarb, sliced
100g soft butter
125g sugar, plus 1 tbsp for sprinkling
¾ tsp vanilla seeds
2 eggs
100ml whole milk
180g all-purpose flour
1 tsp baking powder

Instructions:
Butter and flour a square 20x20cm cake tin and preheat the oven to 180°C. Cream the butter and sugar with a standing or handheld mixer until pale and creamy. Add in the vanilla and eggs one by one while continuing to beat. Add the milk and whisk again. Fold in the flour and baking powder until

you get a smooth batter. Pour the batter into the tin and top with the rhubarb, gently pressing it into the batter with the back of a spoon. Scatter with the sugar. Pop into the oven and bake for approx. 35 minutes or until a skewer inserted in the center comes out clean. Allow to cool slightly before cutting into 9 squares.

Bistro at home

There's nothing as delightful as a few hours spent with good company at a French bistro. These friendly restaurants, the beating heart of the good life in France, are known for their laid-back atmosphere and simple, well-prepared classic dishes. In addition to French culinary favorites such as steak-frites and moules marinères, there is often a *plat du jour* or a two or three-course *menu du jour* on offer for lunch in the afternoon. Wine can be purchased by the bottle or in carafes (a *pichet*) of either a liter, a half liter or a quart, and meals are ended with *un p'tit café* or a *digestif* such as an Armagnac or a Whiskey. *Parfait*!

For a real taste of France at your own table, here are a few tips to create the perfect bistro atmosphere.

- Set the table with a red-and-white checkered tablecloth, and keep the decor simple and rustic. A single flower in a glass vase in the daytime and perhaps a thick candle atop a plain white stand in the evening.
- Always have two carafes on the table: one with water and the other with a smooth

red wine or crisp white wine, depending on the type of food you are serving. Great choices would be Merlot or Sauvignon Blanc.
- In France, bread is a part of every meal. After taking your order, the first thing the waiter will bring you is a carafe of water and a small basket of sliced bread (usually baguette). The bread is *not* meant to be eaten before your meal, but rather *with* your meal. Though some consider it bad etiquette, it is perfectly normal to use a piece of bread to clean your plate – a real delight if you are eating a dish with a beautiful French sauce! Pretty wicker bread baskets are inexpensive and can be found at most home shops. To give your basket a special touch, line it with a white linen napkin. Note that butter is not part of the French bread basket served with meals! And if you're eating out in France, it's perfectly acceptable to ask for more bread.
- Play some classic French *chansons*. Anything by Edith Piaf, Charles Aznavour, Gilbert Bécaud or Charles Trénet would be an excellent choice.
- When in France, visit antique/brocante shops, and if you see a sign pointing to a *vide-grenier* (flea market/garage sale), follow it immediately! Most of my plates, bowls, glasses and cutlery are pre-loved items full of charm and history. Imagine all the amazing French meals that were enjoyed with those very spe-

cial pieces!
- Why not officially declare Saturday evening 'Bistro Evening' for you and your partner? Feed the children early and enjoy a quiet, romantic meal for two! Make the evening last extra long by offering a simple starter and either a dessert or a small cheese platter with some fresh grapes or pears to finish.

Hamburgers on brioche with bacon & confit d'oignons

As much as my daughter enjoys escargots, foie gras on brioche and duck confit, whenever we eat out in France, she will more than likely order a hamburger. A fondness she probably inherited from her father, who is also quite partial to a good, juicy burger. But before you judge, remember that not all burgers are created equal. There is a huge difference between a soggy burger made with a much too salty patty and a gloriously towering burger made with quality beef and fine ingredients.

The following burger is a true culinary beauty. The combination of sweet brioche, smoky bacon and tangy onion confit will leave your palate swooning. I would not serve this with fries. Much too ordinary for a classy burger such as this one.

Note: You will find the recipe for my *confit d'oignons* in *Market Fresh Cooking*, but you can also use a good-quality store-bought onion confit.

Serves 4

Ingredients:
650g good quality, organic ground beef
1 ½ tsp onion powder
1 ½ tsp dried parsley
2 garlic cloves, pressed
1 large egg, whisked
4 tbsps breadcrumbs
Salt (preferably *fleur de sel*) and fresh pepper
Olive oil
4 brioche buns
8 slices streaky bacon
4 tbsps truffle mayonnaise
Greens of your choice
4 tbsps *confit d'oignon*

Instructions:
In a large bowl, knead the ground beef, onion powder, dried parsley, garlic, egg, breadcrumbs and salt and pepper. Shape the mixture into 4 large burgers and let them rest in the fridge for at least 1 hour. Heat the oil in a frying pan and fry the burgers on both sides to your liking. In the meantime, toast the brioche in the oven and crisp up your bacon in an ungreased frying pan. Cut the brioche buns open and spread 1 tbsp truffle mayo over each brioche, top with the burger and bacon, follow with the arugula and *confit d'oignon* and serve.

Cassolette de la mer

Though the name of this dish suggests something utterly fancy, fear not, This aromatic seafood stew makes an impressive main course for a dinner party, but is also a quick and easy weekday meal.

Serves 4

Ingredients:
250g salmon
600 ml fish stock
Good pinch of saffron
Knob of butter
1 tbsp mild olive oil
1 shallot, finely chopped
3 cloves of garlic, finely chopped
500g fruits de mer
100ml white wine
250g shrimp
1 tsp dried dill
Pinch of turmeric
100ml single cream

Instructions:

Poach the salmon in the stock and cut into large pieces. Reserve 500ml of the stock and soak the saffron in about 2 tbsps once cooled. Heat the butter and oil in a large casserole and gently sweat the shallots and garlic. Increase the heat, add the fruits de mer and toss for about 2 minutes. Deglaze with the wine. Now add the salmon back in along with the 500ml reserved stock, shrimp, dill, turmeric and cream. Let the dish cook for another few minutes. Serve with lemon wedges, crisp seasonal vegetables and a nice Riesling.

Moules marinières

Mussels are easy to prepare and delicious in many ways. For the classic *moules marinières*, butter, white wine and parsley are the most important ingredients.

Note:
Rinse the mussels with cold running water before cooking and make sure they are tightly closed (alive). If they are somewhat open, tap them with the back of a knife. If they don't close, discard them. Also discard mussels that are broken. And don't eat mussels that stay closed after cooking.
Serve the mussels with fries or baguette.
The mussels do not need salt. They are salty enough on their own.
Always serve your mussels with a spoon. The cooking juices are absolutely delicious.
You will need a large pan with a lid.

Serves 4

Ingredients:
2 kilos mussels

40g butter
1 onion, finely chopped
2 celery ribs, peeled and finely chopped
2 garlic cloves, finely chopped
1 bay leaf
300ml dry white wine
Flat-leaf parsley, finely chopped

Instructions:

Rinse the mussels and discard any that are dead (they will be open and do not close when tapped with a knife) or broken. Melt the butter in a large pan and gently sauté the onion, celery and garlic for approx. 5 minutes. Increase the heat and add the mussels, bay leaf and white wine. Cover with a lid and allow the mussels to steam for 5-7 minutes, shaking the pan every now and then so that they cook evenly. Take the pan off the heat, stir the parsley through the mussels and serve with either fries or baguette.

Pork loin in lavender & mustard sauce

The following recipe is based on a dish I tried at a restaurant in Le Touquet-Paris-Plage, a handsome seaside town in northern France and the hangout of wealthy Parisians. I would have never imagined that the combination of mustard and lavender would be so sublime. Though not very elegant, I recommend you serve the dish with thin-cut fries, exactly as I ate it at that restaurant.

Note: Make sure to take the pork loin out of the fridge an hour before cooking it and dry the meat well with kitchen paper.

Serves 4

Ingredients:
Knob of butter
2 tbsps olive oil
Salt (preferably *fleur de sel*) and fresh pepper
500g pork loin
375ml strong chicken stock

1 tsp dried lavender
1 tbsp mustard
80ml single cream

Instructions:

Melt the butter with the olive oil in a frying pan. Season the meat with salt and pepper and brown it quickly on all sides. Turn down the heat a little and cook the pork loin for approx. 12-15 minutes, turning it halfway through. Remove from the pan, place on a plate and cover with aluminum foil. Deglaze the pan with the chicken stock. Stir in the lavender and mustard and allow the sauce to cook for 3 minutes before stirring in the cream. Sieve the sauce through a fine mesh colander and return to the pan to reduce for another 3 minutes. Carve the pork loin into 2cm slices, place on a serving platter and drizzle with the sauce. Serve with thin fries and a simple green salad.

Goat's cheese & onion confit tarts

This easy recipe is a delicious start to any summer dinner party.

Serves 4 (multiply recipe as needed)

Ingredients:
4 small square sheets of puff pastry (approx. 15x15cm)
4 thin slices bacon or pancetta
4 tbsps onion confit of choice
Soft, creamy goat's cheese
A little milk, to brush the tarts with
Few handfuls of mixed salad leaves
Balsamic cream, to drizzle

Instructions:
Preheat the oven to 220°C and allow the sheets of puff pastry to thaw if frozen. Put a slice of bacon on each sheet and follow with the onion confit and the goat's cheese. Bring the four corners of the pastry squares toward the center and brush the surface with a little milk. Bake the tarts for approx 12-15 minutes until golden. Serve the warm tarts on a bed of salad drizzled with sweet balsamic syrup.

They are lovely with a dry white or a fragrant rosé.

Salad with apple, ham & mustard vinaigrette

As much as I love cooking, when the weather is truly unbearably hot (as it can get in southwest France), only a salad that requires minimum fuss will do. This is exactly that kind of salad. With fresh baguette and a bottle of chilled white wine, you've got yourself a great summer meal.

Serves 2

Ingredients:
6 leaves radicchio
6 leaves romaine lettuce
Leaves from 1 small bunch of flat-leaf parsley
1 small red apple, cored & sliced
1 tsp Dijon mustard
1 tbsp cider vinegar
3 tbsps olive oil
Salt (preferably *fleur de sel*) and fresh pepper
6 slices dried ham
2 tbsps pine nuts

Instructions:

Wash the lettuce leaves and spin them dry. Tear them and arrange on a large serving platter. Scatter with the parsley and apple. To make the vinaigrette, place the mustard in a small bowl and whisk in the vinegar. Season with salt and pepper. Slowly whisk in the oil until the mixture emulsifies. Pour over the salad. Drape the ham slices over the salad. Toast the pine nuts in an ungreased frying pan, scatter over the salad and serve.

Tarte flambée

Alsace encompasses the Bas-Rhin and Haut-Rhin departments in the Grand-Est region and is nestled between the Rhine River to the east and the Vosges Mountains to the west. The region has alternated between German and French rule several times since the 17th century, and this has resulted in an attractive blend of cultures evident in everything from Alsace's distinct architecture to its culinary traditions. In Strasbourg, the region's cosmopolitan capital and seat of European Parliament, you can delight in traditional cuisine at the many *winstubs*. Literally meaning 'wine room,' these cozy eateries are decked out in nostalgic decor and characterized by their laid-back, convivial atmosphere. Classics include *choucroute garnie* (aromatic sauerkraut) simmered in white wine and abundantly crowned with large chunks of pork, sausages and potatoes); *baeckeoffe* stew; and bacony *flammekueches* (the German name) or *tarte flambée* (the French name).

Come winter, a *tarte flambée* is a perfect and warming weekend lunch. Don't worry about using ready-made dough. It's perfectly acceptable, even in France.

Serves 6

Ingredients:
1 can of ready-made pizza dough
200ml *crème fraîche*
1 ½ tbsp mascarpone
Freshly grated nutmeg
Salt (preferably *fleur de sel*) and fresh pepper
2 onions, halved and thinly sliced
100g lardons
Few sprigs of thyme, leaves plucked

Instructions:
Preheat the oven to 200°C and line a baking sheet with baking paper. Place the dough on the baking sheet and stretch it out as thinly as possible. Mix the *crème fraîche*, mascarpone, nutmeg, salt and pepper. Spread this evenly over the dough. Top with the onions, lardons and thyme. Pop in the oven for 20-25 minutes and serve with an aromatic Riesling.

Moelleux au chocolat

These molten chocolate cakes require few ingredients and are perfect for a dinner party. I like to serve my *moelleux au chocolat* warm, preferably with a scoop of salted caramel ice cream or on a pool of *crème anglaise*.

Note: I used small ramequins measuring approx. 6 ½ cm. If using bigger ones, adjust the time as stated in the recipe.

Serves 6
Ingredients:
150g pure dark chocolate
100g butter
Pinch of salt (preferably *fleur de sel*)
2 eggs, plus 2 egg yolks
120g sugar
50g all-purpose flour

Instructions:
Preheat the oven to 210°C and butter your ramequins well. Place them on a baking sheet covered with aluminum foil. Melt the chocolate, butter

and salt (making sure to grind it finely between your fingers) au bain-marie and allow this mixture to cool slightly. In a small bowl or glass jug, whisk the eggs and the yolks well. Add the sugar and whisk again. Whisk in the flour followed by the chocolate and butter mixture. Divide the batter over the buttered ramequins and bake for approx. 9-12 minutes, depending on the size of your ramequins.

To serve, place a small plate over the ramequin and carefully (using oven gloves if still hot), flip the whole thing over and shake gently until they are released on the plate. You may have to use the tip of a small knife to help them a little.

About the Author

Paola Westbeek grew up in New Jersey and moved to the Netherlands in 1997. She is a food, wine and travel journalist with a huge passion for good eating and all things French. Besides regularly contributing to publications such as Living France, France Magazine, Bouillon and En Route, she has a culinary column on French food history in En Route and one on regional food in Living France. More than 350 of her recipes were published in the popular Dutch women's weekly Vriendin. Paola currently divides her time between France and the Netherlands.

Previously published:
Market Fresh Cooking: A Taste of the French Countryside (2019)
My Winter Kitchen: Warming Recipes for the Cold-

est Months (2019)
Dishing it Up: The Story Behind Twenty Icons of French Food & Drink (2020)

Printed in Great Britain
by Amazon